A MEDAL FOR MARIGOLD
Seattle's Marine Medic

By Michael Skalley
from the journals of Captain Robert Skalley

SUPERIOR PUBLISHING COMPANY
P.O. Box 1710, Seattle, Washington 98111

THE AUTHOR

Michael Skalley, a native Seattleite, has been in the marine scene both ashore and afloat for most of his thirty years, so writing of ships, the people, and action at sea comes naturally. When only twelve years old he put out a newsletter "Talk Between Ships" (ship's anecdotes). Later he made up a weekly report, "Vessel Movements" (information gleaned from ship radio broadcasts). Then came "Logbook Stories" (life and trips aboard ocean tugs). All for private distribution.

After college his marine interests were fixed at Foss Launch & Tug Company where he is now a Section Manager. With full appreciation of the tugboat material at hand, his first major literary effort after two years of research was the story "Foss: Ninety Years of Towboating" a recent and popular Superior publication.

It would follow that Michael Skalley's deep interest in seafaring would find expression again. The material for his second book, the unique *Marigold* story, came from first-hand journals of Captain Robert Skalley, the *Marigold's* Master and a close relative of the author.

THE COVER

The USAHS *MARIGOLD* as depicted on the front cover has been reproduced from an original oil painting by noted marine artist Thomas Wells. The artist remembered passing *MARIGOLD* during the war in the Caribbean. He was a crew member of the barque *PASSAT* at the time.

Library of Congress Cataloging in Publication Data
Skalley, Michael R., 1951–
　　A Medal for Marigold.

　　1. World War, 1939–1945—Medical care—United States.
2. Marigold (Ship)　3. World War, 1939–1945—Hospitals—United States.　　I. Title.
D807.U74M377　1982　　　940.54'76373　　　82–19151
ISBN 0–87564–226–8

COMMENTARY

We had the opportunity to read Michael Skalley's latest book *Medal for Marigold* while still in manuscript form and we enjoyed every page.

The story of the Red Cross ship and her personnel is engrossing and informative. There are no doldrums. The action is relevant and significant. The reader can draw many timely conclusions from the consequences of the events that faced the ship and her marine medics during her travels and in serving the WWII fronts.

We liked the unusual and the unexpected developments in the story— some amusing, some sobering. For interesting and easy reading, a *Medal for Marigold* is well worthwhile.

J J Dillon

Puget Sound Maritime Historical Society

AUTHOR'S FOREWORD

As the *Marigold*, Seattle's only mercy ship, came into being under the auspices and efforts of so many Seattle people, the author, aware of a fund of material about the *Marigold*, was inspired to write up the ship's contribution in WWII as a compliment to the *Marigold's* founders.

The journal of the *Marigold's* Captain, from which this story was taken, was in narrative form including comments, conversations, orders and disclosures. Therefore, where fitting, parts of the narrative are presented in dialogue to enhance a particular scene.

Fortunately, the journals were virtually complete, but where wartime deletions occurred, publications of the *Naval Institute Proceedings* were used to provide dates and facts.

Also fortunately, the Captain was available for interviews and his comments and additions helped to bring the *Marigold* book and her people into living perspective.

The story by its very nature and style and material gives the *Marigold* a personality and creates a bond between personnel and ship. Naturally enough, during the writing of the *Marigold's* life, the author, too, became part of the enduring bond.

A Ballad for *Marigold*

*   *   *

O Lord bless the trips of our hospital ship
A Red Cross marks her snowy white sides
For mercy to all is the *Marigold*'s call
As she sails on the waters worldwide . . .

Sail . . . sail on the waves
Where the whales and the porpoises play
Where never is heard a disparaging word
And the skies light up *Marigold*'s way . . .

*   *   *

Where giving a hand by a devoted band
Of good doctors and nurses and crew
Make our *Marigold* fair an island of care
Midst the flotsam and jetsam of war . . .

Sail . . . sail on the Waves
Where the whales and the porpoises play
Where never is heard a disparaging word
And the stars light up *Marigold*'s way . . .

*   *   *

O ship sail back then with our heroic men
And their valor to heaven do send
As a hard won peace is by sacrifice made
For the land of the free and the brave . . .

Sail . . . sail on the waves
Where the whales and the porpoises play
Where never is heard a disparaging word
And the sun lights up *Marigold*'s way!

written by a Nurse of the 7th Army
aboard the *Marigold* enroute
Naples to the war zone.
August, 1944.

CHAPTER

I

Quite naturally there are unsung heroes in every military conflict and earning a place among them is Seattle's own hospital ship *Marigold* personifying many Seattle people and people from many states—a wide range of talents working together to protect America's heritage. They were the hard hats in the shipyards who converted her from a cruise ship into a modern medical center afloat; they were the women's clubs in an outpouring of effort to finance the ship; they were the Army Medical complement that was the heart of the mercy mission; and they were the Army Transport Service personnel who ran the ship through the thick and the thin of the Mediterranean and the South Pacific fronts in World War II.

The *Marigold*, in 1943, joined a select group, the distinguished marine medics, unique vessels playing an essential role in military conquests originating on enemy-held shores—a vital part of all U.S. liberating campaigns. Though all hospital ships were equipped to specialize in treating casualties fresh from the fronts and transporting them to base hospitals at locations safe from attack, the *Marigold* was the only ship at the time staffed and equipped as a complete general hospital. Her size and facilities made her especially suited for long ocean passages with hundreds of patients requiring continuous and special treatment.

As an expedient, all the Army's early hospital ships were former passenger vessels—their cabin superstructure converting readily to wards and auxilliary rooms. The future *Marigold*, being ideal for conversion, was requisitioned out of a much easier life. She had a sacrifice to make in joining the Army.

Her career at sea started as a first-class liner for the Eastern Steamship Company of New York carrying passengers and freight to and from Europe.

Then she joined the Dollar Steamship Company on their round-the-world service. During World War II, the Army chartered her and the American President Lines operated her to carry troops and supplies to Alaska during the defense of the Aleutian Islands. While taking part in replusing the Japanese attack on Dutch Harbor in 1943, her anti-aircraft guns shot down two enemy fighter planes and one torpedo bomber. In retaliation, Jap pilots subjected her to strafing attacks, inflicting scars she carried for the rest of her days. Even the pilothouse engine room telegraph showed dents from Japanese machine gun bullets. Unfortunately, but necessary, three Japanese trophy flags painted on the bridge wings—attesting to the prowess of the ship's gun crew—were scraped off when she became the *Marigold*.

As a liner, she sailed under three different names. At the New York Shipbuilding Company, where she was built, the government christened her *Old North State* (North Carolina); then she honored two U.S. presidents by becoming the *President Van Buren* and later on the *President Fillmore* (significantly, the best looking of all the presidents), ending up as the U.S.A.H.S. *Marigold*. Fortunately, through all the name changes and changes in service, her fine hull lines were never altered. They were well-displayed in an overall length of 523 feet and her superstructure, well proportioned, remained pleasing to the eye. With her extensive internal space, the gross tonnage totaled a substantial 12,300. Built with twin screws and reciprocating steam engines of 7,000 horsepower, the *Marigold* steamed at thirteen knots and the fuel tanks held sufficient oil for forty-two days of continuous running. Her high-yield evaporators were designed to produce 160 tons of fresh water each day and their output, plus 3,000 tons in tanks, adequately provided for the ship's heavy consumption of water.

For safety at sea she carried twenty-four completely equipped life-boats, including extra blankets, with a total capacity of 1,152—sufficient for everyone aboard. Two boats were motor-propelled and twenty-two, also having propellers, were hand-activated by a system of handles, rods and gears. The hand-propelled boats were built by the Tregonning Boat Works in Seattle, having in mind handicapped patients able to move a handle but unable to pull a heavy oar. The *Marigold*'s long house structure, 225 feet, provided upper deck space to carry the twenty-four lifeboats and their launching davits. For additional capacity, mounted along the main deck, were twelve life rafts and twenty-two life floats, certified to carry 670 persons. The *Marigold*'s safety-at-sea equipment was new, extensive, first quality, and provided a feeling of confidence.

Then, to assure protection from enemy attack and to positively identify the vessel as a hospital ship, the painting and lighting scheme followed the requirements of the Geneva-Hague Red Cross Conventions applying to mercy ships.

What became known as the Geneva Convention was the result of a meeting and agreement of twenty-five countries concerned with the humane treatment of the wounded in land warfare. The Convention, held in 1864 at Geneva, Switzerland, defined rules for caring for and protecting the wounded. It was the beginning of the International Red Cross organization and the final adoption of the Red Cross flag. To further solidify and extend the coverage to other fields, conventions were held in 1899 and 1907 at Hague, Netherlands. At the 1907 meeting, sea warfare was put under the protective rules of the conventions and the international agreements. Ever since, all hospital ships have operated according to the terms and regulations of the conventions and under the sign of the Red cross.

To conform, the *Marigold*'s five crosses were red, the striping green, the hull and superstructure white. Red lights outlined the smokestack cross and the large horizontal cross on the boat deck. Floodlights lit up the funnel and the painted crosses on the ship's sides aft of the bridge. Except in fog, the *Marigold* could never be mistaken for a combat or supply ship, and the conventions under which she operated classed her as immune from attack. Her distinctive markings were her only protection, since she did not travel in convoys or accompany other ships. A self-reliant, independent vessel. However, she was subject to boarding by the enemy to search for combat personnel or offensive arms or supplies in violation of the Geneva-Hague Convention. Due to the right of search, the *Marigold* did not carry radar. As in the case of the Japanese, their sets at the time could display images, but not range, and to protect American technology from easily falling into enemy hands, hospital ships were not permitted the advantages of radar.

All the *Marigold*'s personnel were classed non-combatant, so the hospital complement wore the caduceus badge of the Medical Corps on their Army uniforms and the ship's operating crew, all from the Seattle Port of Embarkation, wore the ship's wheel insignia and the uniform of the Army Transport Service. Almost 400 hands were required to man the ship: 144 ATS crewmen, 4 ATS accountants, 4 signal corps, radio operators, a hospital complement of 18 doctors, 37 graduate nurses, 2 dentists, a veterinarian (food inspection), 1 dietician, a Red Cross supervisor, 6 Medical Corps administrators, 166 medical attendants, and providentially, 2 chaplains.

Appropriately, the Army 212th Hospital Ship Complement drew its personnel from all over the country. Of the thrity-seven nurses, twenty were from the midwest, though eighteen states were represented. The doctors' homes were in eight different states, but it took forty states to provide the medical attendants—from California to Florida, from Washington to Maine. Regardless of origin, the *Marigold* was blessed with a high-calibre staff. True professionals; time, tide, travel and travail would not phase them.

With a complete hospital to look after and a capacity of 765 beds, there would be little idle time for a hospital complement of only 230, a bare minimum, but being highly skilled made up for the lack of numbers. All the *Marigold*'s doctors and nurses came from established private practices—no ninety-day wonders. As time proved, they knew their work and no surprises or situations came up that they couldn't handle, personal or professional. Their contribution to the armed forces was somewhat after-the-fact in view of the *Marigold*'s particular mission, but it was this essential work that made possible, in so many instances, the return of others for the plaudits of a grateful nation.

Thankfully, the staff's overall task was made easier by the outstanding results of the shipyard's conversion and conditioning; in fact, all the installations and equipment functioned as intended, a compliment to the yard crews. The *Marigold*'s personnel many times felt grateful to the men at the Todd Shipyard in Seattle and the Seattle-Tacoma Shipyard in Tacoma for their superlative work in preparing the ship for its special mission. However, much credit is due the personnel of the Seattle Port of Embarkation's Water Division. The section under Lt. Colonel John Barthrup, Superintendent, was responsible for the *Marigold*'s conversion, with Major Rowe of the Maintenance and Repair Department in direct charge, ably assisted by Lieutenant Murray. Due to their close supervision and timely planning, they contributed greatly to the ship's overall excellence.

The Captain, Chief Engineer and Chief Steward were assigned to the *Marigold* when the Army requisitioned her and they followed the conversion from start to finish, organizing and programming the operating departments as work progressed. The Captain, Robert M. Skalley, transferred from Army Transport Service piloting to the *Marigold*.

One of the Army's particular requirements for master of the *Marigold* was administrative proficiency and experience. Captain Skalley's supervisory, organization and instruction work for the Port before being assigned to ships was a deciding factor in Colonel Raymond Hicks Assistant Chief of the Army's Water Division, approving his appointment. After an inspection of the *Marigold*, he said in a few but meaningful words, "The ship is yours; take good care of her, she's very valuable." Brief as the Colonel's instructions were, the Captain never forgot their import.

The Chief Engineer, Harry Johnson, many years a chief, left the transport *David W. Branch* to join the *Marigold* and Bert Williams, an ATS steward before the war, transferred from the San Francisco Port of Embarkation to run the steward's department. With the Captain, they could see the *Marigold*'s coming new look and interior design from blueprints sent the shipyard from Washington. Visualizing what they would have to work with made forming a plan of operation much easier.

Todd removed all the ornamental interior woodwork and most of the cabin bulkheads before starting installation of hospital-type compartments and so the Captain lost his fine office and quarters to the stripping crew the second month of conversion. The Captain's bedroom, sitting room and office had been paneled in birdseye maple with Honduras mahogany trim and the red plush furniture and the large four-poster bed had made the cabin look like a Waldorf suite. But wood paneling in a hospital ship, from a fire-protection standpoint, constituted a definite hazard, so the maple and all the woodwork throughout had to go and be replaced by fire-resistant material.

It was well known that the former captain of the ship, when on round-the-world service, took great delight in his quarters and in the amenities of life. Even his dress was impressive. He wore a short black and red cape over a gold-braided uniform and his cap had a much wider crown than average. Add a pointed beard with hair a bit long for those days and the overall effect was sensational. Quite unusual for the man in command. When asked, Captain Skalley said he had no intention of imitating the showy captain; a hospital ship was a service ship, not a luxury liner.

Shortly after reducing the master's lavish quarters and all the interior bulkheads to bare steel, Todd realized that, with so much naval construction under way at the Seattle yard, they could not assign over 500 men to the *Marigold* job. And with the ship scheduled for delivery by June 1st, at least 1,000 men would be necessary to complete the conversion. Todd knew just what to do to get faster action; they transferred the ship to their Tacoma yard. Two thousand men, designers, fitters, welders, plumbers, electricians, machinists, engineers, painters—all the crafts working around the clock at the Seattle-Tacoma Shipyard—took over the project under Al McNeil, superintendent.

When the ship arrived in Tacoma, the yard generously provided the Captain with an office close to the outfitting pier. The office proved a real boon, what with the many recommendations and special reports to make up, principally the weekly progress report from a seaman's standpoint, to Colonel Barthrup. And with the ship-revamping affecting every foot of space, the office provided a quiet place for the ship's officers to do their paper work and hold planning sessions.

Instead of sending out a summarized progress report to Colonel William H. Schowengerdt, who had recently arrived at Fort Lawton to command the 212th Hospital Ship Complement, the Captain drove out to personally report on the conversion and particularly to meet the Colonel and members of his staff.

The very earnest girl driving the Army car on the thirty-four-mile run to the Seattle fort had little to say other than, "Yes, sir," so the Captain spent the time mulling over one of his unsolved problems—ways and means of handling patients in emergencies. Thinking about the need for instruction reminded him of his last trip to Fort Lawton over a year ago to give one of his lectures to 1,000 troops about to sail to Alaska. Just before every transport departed, the GIs were given a talk on safety at sea and what to expect aboard a ship and in Alaska. Invariably, the first question asked after a very practical speech was what were the girls like in the Aleutians and the answer always produced 1,000 groans. Girls were non-existent except in a few isolated Aleutian families. Then the Captain, trying to look serious, predicted that the frequent howling gales would drive out romantic feelings. The response was as expected—immediate, loud, derisive—and it adjourned the meeting, but on a jovial note.

Finding the Colonel in a conference room with some of his staff doctors and nurses, the Captain's quick impression was that he looked well suited for the job. He was gracious, reserved, but with a ready smile. The doctors—Captain Beebe, Smoloroff, Gaynes, Gradinger and Jones—even without the white coats and stethescopes hanging from their pockets, also looked like a capable group of well-set-up, young-middle-aged hospital physicians. They responded with chuckles to the Captain's description of sailors' cures for seasickness. They were going to be good shipmates.

The nurses too were very attentive to all the ship talk, and every incident of the *Marigold*'s rebirth brought smiles and questions but there seemed to be a touch of gravity in their smiles. Four of the nurses were reminders of Joan Blondell—Esther Risdall, Patricia Carey, Mary Stypul and Mary Morehead. Edna Kook, Tennie Oetken, Claire Schultz and Mary Donahoe were more the Mamie Eisenhower type. The Chief Nurse, Captain Gladys Saterbak, and Ethel Clausen and Mildren Robinson, were tall and of statuesque build, very assured looking. Two more nurses came in when the Captain was ready to leave, Mildred Barr and Helen Schuster—girls with good lines and strong features, but nicely arranged. Appealing would be a one-word description of them all. Thirteen of the thirty-seven assigned nurses were present and if the other twenty-four were as personable, the *Marigold*'s patients should be cheered and readily respond to nursing.

The Captain promised to meet the staff on the ship the following week and personally conduct them through all the hospital sections. In return, the Colonel, Captain Jones, and two of the in-charge nurses would take the Captain to the Marine Room in the Olympic Hotel to be in the proper setting to toast the *Marigold*.

In ten weeks the *Marigold* came back to life, her new look and appearance of seaworthiness a compliment to the craftsmanship of thousands of hands ashore and afloat. And the evidence of quality gained many admiring glances, even by navy sailors on nearby transports. Each day, literally hundreds of additions had appeared in the process of becoming a hospital ship. All the work, materials, and equipment were of the best in outfitting every department. The *Marigold* would take a rating of A-1 to sea with her.

The yard's design section gave the Captain an A-1, lifelike, colored crayon drawing of female pulchritude intended to grace the lounge, since the ship had come to life under feminine patronage. The gilded-frame picture for bulkhead mounting was entitled, "Miss Marigold." One of the naval architects, an accomplished artist, displayed charming components and symmetry in his design of a tall willowy figure, narrow amidships, but with generous flare, ample superstructure and outstanding fittings—all draped in a Grecian gauze gown. She wore an officer's cap and her long red-gold hair formed a mantle around her shoulders. With classic features and raised arms in welcome, she received many compliments and she became a sure-fire conversation piece. But "Miss Marigold" resided in the Captain's sitting room, not in his office and not in the lounge where a more Victorian atmosphere prevailed.

After the ship was structurally complete and equipped, the yard conducted a stability test with heavy weights listing the ship. As a result, they cemented in 2,000 tons of iron ore and concrete block ballast in the forward lower holds. The added weight was to give her an easy but limited roll so she could carry her patients in relative comfort, even in rough seas.

During the last weeks of yard work, the ship appeared to be straining at her tie-up lines, restless to leave the pier, to leave the clutter and the clatter, the day and night activity. The call of the open ocean, the freedom of the sea was affecting Captain and crew alike. After months of patient quiescence, the ship suddenly became alive, became a personality, anxious for expression.

The crew understood. It gave them a feeling of affinity. They belonged. The entire ship's crew standing by, waited impatiently for the yard to finish up so they could prepare the ship for commissioning. The Captain by now had the assistance of a chief executive officer, Elmore Maxwell, and six watch officers. Harry Johnson, the chief engineer, and Jack Gosline, first engineer, had ten assistants in charge of the engine, boiler rooms and auxiliary machinery and equipment. Burt Williams, chief steward, and two assistants ran a large department of over fifty men, largely Filipinos, experienced in food handling. Deck, engine, steward and administrative departments had been fully equipped and functional since late May. All that remained was to complete furnishing the hospital, behind schedule due to the usual war-time delays. Some of the medical equipment arrived weeks late.

Even so, all hospital compartments and accommodations were finished and operational on May 31st. Colonel Schowengerdt directed the outfitting of the hospital sections, assisted by Captain Kenneth Beebe, appointed chief of surgery, and Captain Jules Smoleroff, chief of medicine. The goal, to bring all departments to a state of readiness by June 1st, was right on target and with less than the usual new-ship commotion. The *Marigold* was now ready for final inspection, commissioning and viewing in Seattle for the Women's Clubs, her sponsors.

The ship had the whole-hearted good wishes of the women of Seattle through the Bank's Women's Organization and the Women's Clubs of the Women's Division of the King County War Finance Committee. A special plaque aboard the *Marigold* read:

"THIS HOSPITAL SHIP WAS SPONSORED AND
MADE POSSIBLE BY THE WAR BONDS SOLD
BY THE WOMEN OF SEATTLE, WASHINGTON."

The patriotic ladies sold $4 million worth of bonds and the funds were allocated particularly to the *Marigold*. The Banking Committee members were Mrs. Gudrun Baker, Miss Alice Backstrom, Mrs. Ethel Madden, Miss Sarah Patten and Miss Selma Welch.

Seattle women's organizations taking part in the campaign included the Seattle Visiting Nurse Service, Sunset Club, Marine League Corps Auxiliary, Seattle Milk Fund, Order of the White Shrine, Daughters of the Pioneers of Washington, Seattle Chapter of Hadassah, Seattle Historical Society, Seattle Garden Club, National Society of Colonial Dames in Washington, Junior League of Seattle, National Council of Jewish Women, Lady Lions Club, Chinese Group of Seattle, Women of the Seattle Port of Embarkation, Order of the Amaranth, Women's Auxiliary to the King County Medical Society, Ladies of the Elks, Daughters of the Nile, American Women's Voluntary Services, Naval Officers Wives Club and the Red Cross Motor Corps.

Actively assisting Mrs. John Locke, chairman of the Women's Division of the King Couny War Finance Committee, were Mrs. Leslie Ayer, Miss Claire Forbes, Mrs. John Tenneson, Mrs. Cebert Baillargeon, Mrs. Lucy Hofius, Mrs. Dietrich Schmitz, Mrs. Kenelm Winslow Jr., Mrs. Hertha

Cahill, Mrs. Dan Conley, Mrs. Kester Kleinbert, Miss Hazel Blair and Mrs. Donald Drew.

With such a powerful group, backed by the membership of so many concerned organizations, the bond drive couldn't fail—and it didn't. The *Marigold* and her work became a national symbol of the dedication and spirit of the women's clubs of Seattle. Even the flag, waving from the staff at the stern, was presented to the ship by the bank women. In the *Marigold*'s case, using the term "She" when speaking of the ship was natural since she became a reality under femine sponsorship.

Commissioning at the Tacoma yard on June 10th was impressive, with many important guests including Major General Robert H. Lewis, Commanding General of the Northwest Sector; Colonel Max W. Sullivan, Commanding Officer of Fort Lewis; Colonel M.D. Mills, Commanding Officer of the Mt. Rainier Ordnance Depot; Harold Swan, British Consul; Dr. Kiang Yi-Seng, Chinese Consul; Ross Cunningham, representing Governor Arthur Langlie, and City Councilman Frank J. Laube, representing Mayor William Devin; R.J. Lamont, President of Todd Pacific, and O.A. Tucker, Vice President and General Manager of the Tacoma Division; and representatives of the Bank Women of Seattle, the women's division of the King County War Finance Committee, and the Women's Clubs of Seattle—all wishing the *Marigold* and crew, "God Speed." The medical and ship's officers, in full uniform, stood at attention on the ship's afterdeck for the reading of the Certificate of Commissioning, signed by the Secretary of War and the Secretary of State. Then the Port Commander, General Eley Denson, turned the ship over to Captain Skalley with orders to proceed to Pier A, Seattle Port of Embarkation to complete outfitting before sailing to Charleston, South Carolina for further orders. The Red Cross flag now waved in the breeze from the main–mast; the *Marigold* was in commission.

The trip to Seattle was to be the one and only trial run, everyone confident all would go well. Nevertheless, if assistance was required, two Miki-type large army tugs, one on each side, acted as escorts. The Army allowed newspaper reporters and photographers to ride the tugs to Seattle, so excellent underway pictures appeared in the papers. They gave the purchasers of *Marigold* bonds evidence that their ship had come to life in grand style after months lying dormant. Everything ran smoothly until five miles from Tacoma; then the steering mechanism failed and the ship drifted until trapped air could be worked out of the hydraulic system between pilothouse and steering engine. The delay of two hours was not wasted; half of the equipment check-off list had been initialed as satisfactory by the time the ship was under way. The logbook entry for arrival read: "Fast alongside Pier A, 1700 hours." Only Port employees were on hand to greet the ship, but there was no lack of numbers or enthusiasm.

The Army held open house aboard the *Marigold* on the second night in Seattle. With all deck lights and Red Cross lights burning brightly and the white paint glistening, she made a lasting impression of her importance on the hundreds of eager visitors taking in everything about the ship. After all, they had a vested interest in the *Marigold*.

The hospital staff and the ship's officers, in complete uniform, were on hand to accompany members of the Women's Clubs and other guests and to explain the *Marigold*. The Captain at the foot of the gangway and the Colonel on the deck greeted each visitor as they arrived and if they were sponsors they were directed first-off to the women's plaque presented to the ship.

The medical attendants acted as tour guides and the question repeatedly asked them after noticing the *Marigold*'s high sides was how patients were brought aboard. The medics, litter bearers when the ship loaded patients, explained that the ship had side ports (doors) to allow the entry of gangways to walk up on or carry litters aboard. And there were accommodation ladders (stairways) port and starboard which could be lowered from the main deck to the water. Then at times the ship's gear (derricks) would be used to hoist litters aboard from ambulance ships pulled alongside. Ambulatory patients would of course walk aboard and litter cases would be carried to the wards. The medics added that all patients would have a tag showing condition and treatment administered by field units. The *Marigold* would take care of casualties, like any shore hospital, until they were transferred to a base hospital.

The question most frequently asked the Captain was whether hospital ships had ever been attacked. The answer was yes in World War I, but no in the present war. However, two British ships did suffer damage, which was claimed to be accidental, and the Captain explained that it could happen when hospital ships worked in areas where enemy bombing occurred.

Some of the women visitors wondered about the discomfort of seasickness to the wounded. The deck officers were usually asked the question and they said it was a real cause for concern and it had been discussed at length with the Captain, and that avoiding rough weather or putting the ship in the most favorable position to the sea were the only practical alternatives.

Three of the congenial, in-charge nurses—Esther Risdall, Ethel Clausen and Mildred Robinson—were asked many times by the younger visitors if they would have preferred shore duty where there would be more recreation. The answer was no, because they all had applied for ship duty—the choice was theirs and, as they had expected, friendships were much closer and they found greater unity of purpose than in a shore hospital. The lieutenants made a particular point of explaining that they joined the ANC solely to take care of casualties and that they knew from experience army nursing was demanding work but, like any other profession, there was time for relaxing. The nurses intentionally went into detail on the many compensations, hoping the young girls would be impressed and go into career nursing.

Particular interest was shown in the operating rooms—Captain Beebe and Captain Jones answered the questions. The dentist's office had Captain Wilkens in charge, and the chaplains, medics and stewards answered questions in the chapel, ship's stores, pharmacy, laundry, galley and bakery. The guests soon realized the *Marigold* was in all respects self-sufficient—a complete home away from home for the patients and the personnel.

For those guests looking in on the chapel and inclined to visit, the ship's Catholic chaplain, Captain Mieczkowski, gave them some surprising facts on the origin of the Red Cross and its early use as a symbol of compassion and relief. The cross was first formed by a religious order in Naples, Italy—Servants of the Sick—in the sixteenth century, headed by Camillus De Lellis, later to become a canonized saint. The order, then as now, wore a black cassock, and in 1586 Pope Sixtus granted them the privilege of wearing a cross of red cloth on their habit. The cross served as a reminder to those who wore it of their commitment of service to the sick, and they used it to invoke in the sick, feelings of faith, hope and confidence as they recalled the sacrifice of the Lord—resulting in remarkable natural healing and outright miracles.

The Camillians, as they are known, considered the red cross a sign of Christian charity 300 years before the formation of the International Red Cross. And even though the International Red Cross flag is the Swiss flag with the colors reversed, the significance of the red cross has remained since its inception—care of the afflicted.

And, yes, the Chaplain did have the Society's crosses; they were made of red wool, one inch in size. It would be most appropriate for a patient to wear a red cross on a Red Cross ship.

The navigation department on the bridge deck appealed to the men and young boys and they kept Roy Robeck, second officer, and Ray Fosse and Ray Betz, third officers, busy giving descriptions of the equipment. The gyro compass system, master compass, and five repeaters at different locations brought on the most questions and were the hardest to answer because they pointed true north and not magnetic north, like the more familiar compasses. The bridge officers, to give a simple explanation of a complicated mechanism, said the compass rotor turned at 6,000 rpm and a law of physics stated that a rapidly spinning body tended to line up with the poles of the earth. Roy Robeck, in charge of all the navigation equipment, later reported they had 140 visitors and had answered 1,400 questions. Since the officers were all under thirty, they weren't too exhausted.

The ship's whistle sounded several times, either by intent or accident in flipping the control lever on the part of the young guests. It did add a realistic feeling for all the visitors of being aboard a ship. The *Marigold*'s whistle, three feet long, had a deep bass voice. The sound rolled out in easy, almost melodic waves so it was no wonder the whistle had a workout.

The engineers, due to auxiliary machinery in operation, allowed the visitors to view the engine room and boiler room only from the upper gratings, but that satisfied their curiosity. The massive two-deck-high main engines, with their rods, cranks and cylinders, amazed the onlookers. The junior engineer on watch came up and explained the ship had six boilers, 100 inches in diameter, and made with 1–11/16″ plate. They would burn 525 barrels of fuel each steaming day. At 1982 fuel prices, the daily cost would have been $14,700—twice as much as the ship's entire daily payroll at that time.

The practical-minded commented to the medical attendants, stationed in the passageways, on the use of Sea-Por-Cel (trade name), with its porcelain face and asbestos back, as being an ideal fireproof paneling for a hospital ship and also easy to keep clean—it was used throughout the ship. The entire interior appeared light and bright due to the glossy white panels, and the inside decks of red magnesite made a pleasing combination. The visitors agreed the ship was safe, comfortable and hospitable— the bond money had been wisely spent.

The Neuropsychiatric wards, in charge of Captain Ross, psychiatrist, and Lieutenant Patricia Carey, ANC, were down two decks from the main deck, but even so, over one hundred visitors were shown the locked rooms, some padded, some bare and some furnished in normal fashion. There was a consulting room, treatment room with shock equipment, and nurses' station—all completely furnished. Lieutenant Carey explained that ten percent of the casualties would be mental cases and their job would be to get the men back on the beam with as little strain and upset as possible. Most of the disorders would be the result of battle fatigue and fear, ending in an escape from reality. The lieutenant said they wouldn't activate the wards until arrival in the war zone, unless some of the unlucky gamblers on the ship became manic-depressives.

From the many remarks heard as the groups of visitors and sponsors left the ship, there was no doubt they were highly pleased that their bond purchases had gone to provide such a well-found ship. Some of them said, when the war was over, to bring the ship back to Seattle because they were the owners! By 2200 hours the last "Good luck" had been wished and the ship's personnel were free to leave for Fort Lawton and private homes for another night ashore.

Six days later, after all stores and supplies were stowed, the *Marigold* left Pier A, with port officers and a large showing of office personnel on hand to wave bon voyage as she pulled away for Charleston, South Carolina, her new home port. The Captain was especially pleased to see the staff officers from the General Service Section: Major Jennings; his assistants Captain Wright and Lieutenant Gunderson; with Marine Superintendent Captain Shears following along on the pier as the ship backed out of the slip. The officers had provided the *Marigold* with the best of crewmen and equipment. Their particular interest in the alterations to the ship and furthering the captain's recommendations was of inestimable value. The *Marigold* was fortunate in having high-calibre supervisors throughout her conversion.

But before going to sea, a call had to be made at the degaussing range, located ten miles up-Sound from Seattle, to check out the ship's degaussing system. Degaussing cables, running along both sides inside the hull, had been installed to counteract the ship's magnetism and prevent detonating magnetic mines. With the test showing the system functioning properly, the ship moved on to the Point Wells oil dock to take on fuel. Then, twenty hours later on June 18, 1944, with bunkering complete, all personnel accounted for, and the Captain back aboard from the Navy routing office, the *Marigold* headed for sea and a new life.

Since sea watches would not start until dropping the pilot at Port Angeles fifty miles away, the Captain sent the junior officers down to the promenade decks to answer questions on the passing marine traffic, Puget Sound history, and points of interest along the way. The ship's rails were well-filled and the boys later told the Captain no one shed any tears, they were all happy to be a part of the *Marigold*'s complement and glad to be aboard a ship and not an army bus.

CHAPTER

II

E arly in the evening the ship passed Cape Flattery and felt the
motion of the open ocean for the first time in six months. The
Pacific's gentle westerly swell gave her a light rock and roll, just
enough to lull the enthusiastic complement into a sound sleep on their first
night at sea.

Lookouts were alerted to the Navy warning of submarine sightings off
the coast. Previously, the Japanese, with modern submarines and superior
torpedoes, had sunk a number of ships, including four tankers. The subs
had ranged, virtually unopposed, from Cape Flattery to San Diego.

As if on cue, a loud shout broke from the bridge wing, "Submarine to
starboard!" The Captain, with binoculars at the ready, took a quick look.
True, there was a white train on the surface, and made by a column about
three feet high, but it wasn't a periscope. It was the dorsal fin of a killer
whale. The relief on the decks was self-evident. However, when sighted at
dusk or in the track of the moon, the whale could cause instant alarm. But
now in the setting sun a school of black and white whales accompanied the
ship for several miles giving the first-trippers something to watch besides
the rush of white water along the ship's side.

If coming events cast their shadows before them, then with no bad signs
showing, the 4,400-mile run to Panama wouldn't hold any unwelcome
surprises. To the neophytes, if the sea didn't act up it would be a blessing;
they wouldn't suffer from *mal-de-mer* while waiting to get their sea legs,
and no one would say they had six meals a day—three down and three up.
In fact, the *Marigold's* good weather pact with the weatherman had
started.

For the deck officers, by their choice, the blue-sky run south turned into
a time of questions and answers to start the novices thinking fore and aft,
not front and back—bow and stern, not sharp end and blunt end. But for

This photo was taken aboard the *Marigold* enroute to Seattle after the ships commissioning ceremonies. From left, Captain Robert Skalley—master of the *Marigold*, Lt. Col. Barthrup—Superintendent of the water division Seattle Port of Embarkation, H. E. Jamison—newspaper reporter for the Seattle Star. (U.S. Army Signal Corps photo)

THE
Secretary of War

OF

THE UNITED STATES OF AMERICA

does hereby COMMISSION
The
U.S. ARMY HOSPITAL SHIP

"MARIGOLD"

PURSUANT TO THE ARTICLES OF THE "CONVENTION BETWEEN THE UNITED STATES AND OTHER POWERS FOR THE ADAPTATION TO MARITIME WARFARE OF THE PRINCIPLES OF THE GENEVA CONVENTION", THE RATIFICATION OF WHICH BY THE GOVERNMENT OF THE UNITED STATES WAS DEPOSITED AT THE HAGUE ON NOVEMBER 27, 1909, THE WAR DEPARTMENT OF THE UNITED STATES OF AMERICA, ON FEBRUARY 24, 1944, DESIGNATED THE AMERICAN FLAG VESSEL "MARIGOLD" AS A U. S. ARMY HOSPITAL SHIP.

THE WAR DEPARTMENT IS THE OPERATOR OF THE VESSEL, HEREINAFTER CALLED THE "U. S. ARMY HOSPITAL SHIP MARIGOLD," WHICH VESSEL WAS BUILT OF STEEL IN THE YEAR 1920 AT CAMDEN, NEW JERSEY, U. S. A. SAID VESSEL IS A STEAMSHIP OF 11,342 GROSS TONS, HAS A LENGTH OF 502 FEET, HAS 3 SETS KINGPOSTS WITH FORETOPMAST ON TIE GIRDER BETWEEN MIDDLE SET OF KINGPOSTS AND MAINTOPMAST ON TIE GIRDER BETWEEN AFT SET OF KINGPOSTS, ONE FUNNEL, THE LENGTH OF THE FORECASTLE IS 44 FEET, AND THE LENGTH OF THE POOP IS 44 FEET. THE DISTANCE FROM THE BOW TO FORWARD SET OF KINGPOSTS IS 72 FEET, FORWARD SET OF KINGPOSTS TO MIDDLE SET OF KINGPOSTS IS 63 FEET, MIDDLE SET OF KINGPOSTS TO FUNNEL IS 132 FEET, FUNNEL TO AFT SET OF KINGPOSTS IS 164 FEET, AND AFT SET OF KINGPOSTS TO STERN IS 72 FEET. THE AMIDSHIP STRUCTURE IS 255 FEET LONG WITH BRIDGE DECKHOUSE 218 FEET LONG, PROMENADE DECKHOUSE 187 FEET LONG AND BOAT DECKHOUSE 62 FEET LONG ABOVE.

NOTIFICATION OF THE DESIGNATION OF THE "U. S. ARMY HOSPITAL SHIP MARIGOLD" TO BE OPERATED BY THE UNITED STATES ARMY IN ACCORDANCE WITH INTERNATIONAL PRACTICE UNDER THE TERMS OF THE HAGUE CONVENTION X, 1907, WAS DELIVERED TO THE HUNGARIAN AND RUMANIAN GOVERNMENTS ON MARCH 9, 1944, TO THE BULGARIAN AND GERMAN GOVERNMENTS ON MARCH 10, 1944, TO THE JAPANESE GOVERNMENT ON MARCH 11, 1944, AND TO THE THAI GOVERNMENT ON MARCH 18, 1944.

THEREFORE, SAID VESSEL IS ENTITLED TO IMMUNITY AND PROTECTION IN ACCORDANCE WITH INTERNATIONAL PRACTICE AND UNDER THE TERMS OF THE HAGUE CONVENTION X, 1907.

DONE AT THE CITY OF WASHINGTON, THIS TWENTY THIRD DAY OF APRIL IN THE YEAR OF OUR LORD ONE THOUSAND, NINE HUNDRED AND FORTY FOUR, AND OF THE INDEPENDENCE OF THE UNITED STATES OF AMERICA THE ONE HUNDRED AND SIXTY EIGHTH.

ATTEST:

Henry L. Stimson
SECRETARY OF WAR

Cordell Hull
SECRETARY OF STATE

Commissioning Certificate

the Captain, he had programs a little more serious in mind. He started his own question-and-answer series in the form of daily ship inspections at 1000 hours, along with the department heads and their yeomen, questioning and noting items to be corrected or improved. Living areas and all aspects of food handling were given close scrutiny. The inspection was thorough but not the white-glove type.

With the inspection tours underway, the Captain then began a program of fire and boat drills to familiarize everyone with their proper station and assignment. Lieutenant Vaunda Borum was offered the position of fire marshal, her father being fire chief of Aberdeen, Washington. She said she didn't have the regulation hat so would have to decline the honor, but she did give practical suggestions on the care of hoses—always drain and dry canvas hoses before re-reeling. Instructions for drills were posted on printed and framed station bills throughout the ship, covering all crew members.

At the sound of seven short whistle blasts and seven rings on the general alarm bells, all the off-duty ship's crew, with life jackets on, reported to lifeboat stations on the boat deck as ordered on the station bills. The medical complement, with life jackets on, reported to their assigned boat stations on the embarkation deck or their evacuation station in the wards, as the situation required. The crew, having had lifeboat training, handled all boat-launching operations under the direction of the boat officer and on orders from the captain on the bridge. At sea, and for practice only, the top bank of boats were swung out and, weather permitting, lowered to the embarkation station for loading. Only during drills in port were boats put in the water and maneuvered.

However, even with efficiency by constant practice in operating the boats, loading the boats with patients—due to inconstant conditions—never could be perfected. The plan for embarking handicapped patients was complete, but only paper perfect. Having practical plans to act on in emergencies was essential, since there was no guarantee of immunity from the danger of striking floating mines adrift from anchors, navigational hazards or accidental attacks.

The second weekly fire drill, actuated by ringing the general alarm for one minute, turned out to be a real break in ship routine—not a figurative one. During the drill, hoses were water-tested as customary, but this time with fog nozzles (sprayers) attached. Suddenly the hose pressure shot up, straightening out the lines like frozen ropes, causing the hoses to fly out of the relaxed hands of the men holding the nozzles over the sides. The hoses whipped back aboard, twisting and lashing out in wide arcs—confined only by the bulwarks and deck houses. Streams of water shot into open ports and at crew and spectators along the decks. A hurried call to the engine room and the fire pumps stopped. The life went out of the hoses, but not before several broke wide open from the pressure. Wet bunks and clothes were not the only complaints. There was a fresh-water rinsing chore to prevent staining; the hoses spouted salt water. In the track-down, the reason for the wild hoses was a combination of the restrictive fog nozzles and inaccurate low readings on the pump pressure gauges. Corrective calibration eliminated a repetition.

Continuing with the display and the use of safety-at-sea equipment, the Captain had the third officers conduct a Lyle-gun demonstration on the boat deck—a test required by sea law, but one providing an unexpected result.

The small cannon, forged with a thick barrel twenty-four inches long, was used to fire a projectile with a line attached across to another ship or the shore if close. It was the first step in passing heavier lines and rigging a breeches-buoy (canvas bag) to ride on a trolley to transfer people from a ship in distress. The third officers, Ray Fosse and Ray Betz, were the gun-layers because they had recently passed Coast Guard tests that included safety-at-sea equipment. Carl McGee, the boatswain in charge of the seamen, secured the gun from recoiling. The gunners rammed a charge of black powder and wadding down the muzzle and placed a lead slug, with line hooked on, down the elevated barrel. A large group of advisers were on hand to comment on the action. "You couldn't hit the *Queen Mary* with that relic!" "Cannons are *verboten* on a hospital ship!" "Why not fire a harpoon and get a shark, maybe a whale." "Any chance of going deaf?" Art Bratsberg, the chief Army Transportation Service accountant, gave the most fitting advice, "Hang on to the line and save the lead, it's war-time!" In spite of all the pointed advice, the detonator cap was placed in the firing hole and the pull-cord led away from the gun.

With the audience well back and the ship slowed down, Ray Fosse yanked the cord, setting off a report like a car backfiring, and the missile flew out, unreeling the line as it arched over the water. The gun had strained against the hold-down lines, but didn't take off after its detractors. The slug and line angled down toward the ship. Suddenly someone yelled, "There's something on it!" As the line came closer, a life ring came surging through the water, the line right through the center hole—a million to one shot! The audience rushed to the rail, stared fixedly at the half-submerged ring plowing through the water, apparently unable to believe what they were seeing.

A hook line brought up a damaged ring with faint lettering reading *Henry Bergh*; the hailing port looked like San Francisco. Ray Fosse looked around, "How's that for bull's-eye shooting?" The audience gave him a hand and even the detractors wanted another shot, but the gun crew decided to rest on their laurels. Later the Captain checked on the ship and found there was a Liberty ship named *Henry Bergh* which had run aground and broken in half off the Farallon Islands near San Francisco. Fortunately, the 1,000 men returning on the *Bergh* from the South Pacific were rescued without mishap. Since the life ring was too weather-beaten to mount, the gun crew put it around their cabin porthole, proud of their marksmanship. But when Ray Betz later learned he had a nephew in the *Bergh*'s crew, they agreed he should get the souvenir life ring.

One more go-round and sea parlance in four easy lessons would be over. All the watch officers, including the juniors Dick Richings, John Hogan and Rex Harwood, during their off-watches, took part in the important work. They said the landlubbers had the hardest time in keeping from saying downstairs and upstairs instead of down below and topside. Then middle for amidships and across for athwartship and, the most heinous, floor for deck. But a little practice corrected the grave errors and then ship vernacular came easily. The pupils were all anxious to learn. Anxious to be part of the seagoing fraternity. Some of the doctors were too reserved to join in, but most of the staff did; the nurses especially wanted to salt their conversation. The deck officers worked in pairs; what one didn't know the other did. They had an easy time in the conversion except at the final session; two well-read nurses, Avis West and Sissy Klingfelter, almost stumped them with why call the left side port? The sailors had good memories. It used to be called larboard, but sounded too much like starboard. Then, what are holidays aboard ship? Skips and misses left in painting. Why call propellers screws? They work in water like screws in wood. What does the bridge mean? The ship control platform running from one side to the other, including the pilothouse. What are coamings? Raised door sills to keep out sloshing water. On a ship, what's a fashion plate? A steel plate cut in a special shape for good contouring. And why call the Captain the Old Man? In the sailing ship days, he was father to the crew. The girls said, now that they had that explanation, they were going up to the bridge and ask for the "Old Man" and see what happens; they thought the Captain wasn't even thirty-five years old. They did go up and asked the watch officer if they could see the "Old Man." Roy Robeck, on watch, held back a grin, told them to follow the quartermaster. Harry Dolley knocked on the Captain's office door and said, "Two nurses are here and said they want to see the 'Old Man'." At the "Come in," the girls opened the door, looked serious, and said as one, "If you're the old man, who is the old lady?" By the time the Captain, a little taken aback but laughing, reached the door, the girls were already out on deck. If they hadn't bolted he would have answered their question by saying, "The *Marigold*!"

After the vocabulary lessons were over, the Captain no longer winced from abuse of Neptune's language. The officers' cure had been successful and the Captain told them that, if the ship ever crossed the equator and Neptune came aboard to initiate the polywogs, he would put in a good word for them with both Neptune and Davy Jones.

In the meantime, the staff provided some of their own type of action. Each evening on the foredeck the medical personnel enlivened the ship with musical entertainment, both instrumental and vocal. Even the Colonel took over the lead with a good tenor voice whenever his ever-present cigar went out—his favorite song, "The Easter Parade." The strains of "Marie Elena," "Blue Champagne," "Sentimental Journey" and "Red Sails in the Sunset" came across loud and clear with the special goodnight song, "Dream Your Troubles Away," a fitting finale. It was Captain Lanning, the ship's Protestant chaplain, who organized the program, making the evening a time to look forward to with the hour of song and music.

Regardless of all the ship activity, religious opportunities were not neglected. Every morning the Catholic liturgy was offered by Captain Mieczkowski in the *Marigold*'s chapel, and Captain Lanning held services besides Sunday for the other faiths. The two clergymen, ready for private consultations at any time, kept the ship on the spiritual beam. It was better than radar. Their favorite words of guidance were thought-provoking. "When everything else fails, read the instructions—in the Bible!"

Below the after main deck—the crew's quarters—the Filipino members of the steward's department provided their own entertainment with a game called Pai Kow. Because it ran to very high stakes, the stewards had told John Sampson, the head Filipino, to limit the play to his own boys. The game looked innocent enough, with domino-like plaques set up before each player. Dice decided the winning plaques and, like blackjack, it was played against the dealer. Some evenings several hundred dollars changed hands. It was an exciting game, win or lose, so they claimed.

The medical attendants, quartered on A deck forward, had their own style of play going—dice and poker—strictly GI with controlling limits. Technicalities were overlooked for the sake of diversion. The Sergeant-Major, a career man, was generally the high winner; he said his winnings equalled his salary. However, regardless of the amusements, most of the medics were serious about their work and seriously trying to improve their rating. They maintained a good *esprit de corps*, which boded well for the *Marigold*'s mission.

For the ship's officers, quartered on the boat deck and in the main deck house, social activities were curtailed due to the demands of their work—running the ship was a twenty-four-hour job. To remedy the lack, the Captain gave the medical staff free run of the upper decks and in turn the Colonel offered the ship's officers the privilege of visiting in the lounge and on the upper promenade deck, the hospital staff's private domain. The wide teakwood bulwark rail became a favorite fixture to lean on while watching the frothy water go by and keeping up on the latest rumors.

A practical joker in the administrative department came up with a good one; he started a story that the staff living on the starboard side of the promenade deck was far superior to those living on the port side, the reason being that the staterooms on the port side had odd numbers, and so the odd people were put in those cabins! Ridiculous, but nevertheless it made the rounds, and the nurses played it up. Whenever one of the bridge officers, including the captain, stopped by the starboard side and neglected the port, there would be questioning and feigned grim looks when passing or meeting anyone from the port side. The port-siders thought of dressing oddly, but decided the whole thing a bit ludicrous, so the odd and even game closed for want of players.

To everyone's pleasure, and for genuine news and entertaining reading, the Special Services Division of the hospital complement, under the direction of Lieutenant William Senkfor, published a two-page newspaper called the *Portholer*—boasting editorial, art, printing and circulation departments. Regular columnists, Lieutenant Doris Schwartz, Warrant Officer Robert Marks, and ten special contributors helped to keep the *Portholer* lively, particularly Captain Padwosocka, MC, a second Ernie Pyle. And to everyone's further pleasure, there was no advertising and no subscription charge. The paper was an instant success; however, at times its weather prediction section was all wet.

In spite of the *Portholer*, the weather didn't cool down; it got progressively warmer as the *Marigold* steamed south at about 300 miles a day and the dress became more casual. Suntans without ties became the accepted dress for all personnel except the nurses, already in summer dress. They wore white and brown striped seersucker, either dresses or shirt and slacks. The dresses were wrap-around and in a wind could be quite revealing—but they were cooler.

The hot weather off the Lower California coast was helpful for getting used to the expected heat of Charleston, as the summertime temperature there at times reached 104°. Unfortunately, air-conditioning was not common on military vessels, but blowers circulating outside air helped. The personnel coming from the midwest were less troubled by the hot weather than the Puget Sounders, used to the region's cool weather. Heat rash was the first complaint treated aboard the *Marigold*, but the patients were not hospitalized, even for practice.

The Navy's routing held the ship close inshore, sailing from position point to position point. The last one, Cape Mala, the final landfall, was followed by Taboquilla Island in Panama Bay, eight and one-half miles from Balboa, the entrance to the Canal. The anchor dropped in twelve fathoms off the island to await a canal pilot to take the ship through the dredged approach channel. Daily mileage-run betting pools were played on the trip south and the largest pot paid off for the closest time to the second when the anchor hit the water in Balboa Bay. Medic Bill Cannariota of Passaic, New Jersey, pocketed $150.

During the sixteen days to Panama, there was no disappointment that no curious submarines had surfaced for a look at the Army's only hospital ship in the Pacific. With Japanese supply bases so far from the Pacific Coast, there was a good possibility the enemy had abandoned raiding shipping on the West Coast. However, the Germans in the Atlantic and the Caribbean were still looking for prey and in two days the *Marigold* would be in their hunting grounds. Standing orders, calling for a sharp lookout by all three bridge watches, would then be more important than ever.

While waiting for the pilot, the Captain thought of his first of many canal trips, made in pelting rain, spoiling the whole day. It was in 1926 when he was seventeen years old and just out of high school. The ship was the *Heffron* of the Weyerhaeuser Steamship Company, loaded with 5 million feet of lumber for Baltimore. The rain came down in torrents, enough to fill the locks. Then sunshine and more deluge, off and on, all during the transit. But today on the *Marigold* a clear sky, low humidity, a hot sun, all presaged pleasant weather. What a difference! Of course, the *Heffron* didn't have the influence of two clergymen, the merits of thirty-seven Florence Nightingales and the blessings of the women in twenty-two clubs—no wonder the weather was well-behaved.

After a four-hour detention at anchor, the ship got underway for the Balboa fuel dock and proceeded up the straight eight-mile channel, plainly marked by twenty buoys. Everyone off duty lined the rails, decked out in dress khakies, looking forward to Panama City. Once alongside the dock, shore leave was quickly arranged. The canal transit would not be until morning making possible an afternoon and evening in Panama. In high fettle, a stream of uniformed *turistas* poured down the gangway to invade Panama City.

Stores, taxis and bars were well patronized. No doubt the air-conditioning in the bars was the attraction. Free of tax, bottles of perfume or cologne bulged from purses and pockets of returning sightseers. From now on the ship would be fragrant as well as functional. At sun-up a number of bodies were to be seen stretched out on the lawn above the dock. They hadn't quite made the gangway. The cooler outside air and the soft green grass was the reason for the sleep-out—so they maintained.

The Captain, coming on the bridge to fill out the transit papers, noticed the completely relaxed forms on the gentle sloping greensward and prompted a good laugh with Rex Harwood, officer on the four-to-eight watch. Pointing to the recliners, the Captain said, "The scene reminds me of the logbook entries on a freighter tied up at this same dock in the 1920s. The ship's captain, late in the day, had written, 'Mate drunk today'. Later still, the mate read the entry, then put underneath the comment, 'Captain sober today'."

Next morning, with everyone back aboard and the rails filled with absorbed gazers, the ship headed through Balboa Reach, three miles to the Miraflores Locks for the lift of about sixty-five feet; then a mile and a half to Pedro Miguel Lock, a lift of thirty feet; then Cucaracha Reach, the big Culebra Cut and on through ten long tangents twenty-seven miles to Gatun Locks, where the *Marigold* dropped close to ninety feet to the Caribbean Sea level. The short channel, heading north, led to Limon Bay and to an anchorage close to Colon and Cristobal, ending an eight-hour transit.

The Captain had signalled for a shore boat and, as it bumped alongside, he told the railbirds not to pull out and leave him stranded in Cristobal— he was headed for the navy office for briefing and routing. During the session, the wind and sea made up and the captain's boat, returning alongside the *Marigold*, rolled and plunged, making it a risky jump to the Jacob's Ladder swinging twenty-five feet down the ship's side. The watchers above called down, then were silent. The Captain, with a briefcase tucked under an army belt and timing the leap with the rise of the boat, landed on the bottom step, hands grasping the side ropes—then the climb was safe, but wet.

Due to recent torpedo attacks close by, and with high wind and seas stopping periscope work, the Captain was anxious to get as far from the area as possible under the cover of a black night and the safety of heavy weather. Regardless of convention-immunity, a risk always existed, and any evasive tactic lessened the danger.

After clearance by blinker, the ship ran a mile to the net and through the opening between the concrete breakwaters, then out past the sea buoy to head on a northerly course for Jamaica and the Windward Passage between Cuba and Haiti.

Instead of making for the Florida coast, the routing called for a run north through and to a point well clear of the Bahama Islands and wide of the usual steamship tracks—so few ships were sighted. There was a time in 1942 and 1943 when the passage would have been extremely hazardous. Nevertheless, the watch officers were on continuous alert. The Navy warned there were still a few die-hard U-boats operating in the Caribbean, lying in wait for unescorted ships.

Not long before this, the Atlantic Coast sea lanes had been made safe by the convoy system, but unfortunately, convoys were not possible in the early months of the war; the Navy lacked escort vessels. As a result, according to a classified report given the Captain at the Navy Routing Office, the cost in men and ships was appalling. The Navy was unprepared to combat the mass submarine warfare unleashed in January 1942 when Germany sent five of their super U-boats, holding fourteen torpedoes, to the Atlantic Coast and in the first two weeks of attack sank twenty-five ships (200,000 tons). Then, in February, seven more subs were assigned for a blitz in the Caribbean and they immediately bagged seventeen tankers. Moving to the Carolina, Georgia and Florida coasts, they sank 335,000 tons of shipping in one month. In March, nine ships were torpedoed in the Windward Passage. The first-quarter sinkings reached a staggering total of one hundred twenty-eight and, in May, another twenty went to the bottom. By May 1942, twenty-seven U-boats were ranging, practically unopposed, from Canada to the Gulf of Mexico, and the tonnage sunk reached one million! The Kreigsmarine called their operation "The American Turkey Shoot!"

In desperation, the Navy accepted help from British escort vessels to move ships in convoy, and the menace quickly lessened. From August 1942 to May 1943, only a few ships were sunk along the coast, but twenty went down around the Windward Passage on the *Marigold's* route. From June 1943 to May 1945, only four ships were sunk off the Atlantic Coast and twelve in the Caribbean. As more escort vessels and patrol planes became available, the U-boats were driven away to better pickings in the North Atlantic and European coasts. Losing the effectiveness of their subs, the Germans tried mining U.S. harbors; they had little success, and the one hundred twenty ships a day traveling the eastern sea frontier moved in relative safety from U-boat attack or floating mines but, regrettably, the damage had already been done. Naturally the Captain and crew felt a great reverence and sadness knowing they were passing over the final resting place of many victim crews lost with their ships in what was so scoffingly termed a "Turkey Shoot." And, as the miles passed, the conviction grew of the grave need of taking the Coast Guard guideline "always prepared" more seriously.

Each day as the ship came closer to Charleston, speculation aboard increased on the ultimate destination. Would the *Marigold's* mission take her to Africa, Italy, France or some English Channel port? Would she be stationed at beachheads or carry wounded back to the States? Surely the

Charleston orders would be definite, but then, in this war, constant change was the only thing definite—orders changed without notice.

The *Marigold*'s rails were already filling when the obstruction-buoy marking a wreck fourteen miles offshore from the Charleston entrance was sighted. And there were no vacant places by the time the ship made the six-mile run to the range markers along the Cooper River. Nobody left the deck during the four miles to the estuary, passing famous Fort Sumter on the way, and during the ten more miles up the river to the Charleston Army Base. The *Marigold* looked like a troop transport coming in with one side of the decks over-crowded.

Arriving without incident, but not without strain, at 1400 hours on July 11th, the *Marigold* completed a run of 1,800 miles from the Canal. After docking, the pilot pointed out the hospital ship *Seminole* at the next pier and said she had returned with a load of patients from Naples after weeks on a run from Oran and Bizerte in North Africa to Naples. However, the ship's complement was away on leave and this disappointed the *Marigold* staff as they wouldn't be able to get a first-hand report on the Mediterranean action. The practical information would have been extensive since the *Seminole*, a small former coastal liner, had been a mercy ship for a year.

The Army reception and inspection teams waiting on the dock looked surprised at the high number of persons lining the rails. They hurried aboard once the gangway was placed, eager and curious to see what kind of work the West Coast shipyards turned out and why all the personnel. They were pleased with the condition of the ship, the many facilities installed for a complete general hospital, and they quickly understood that a large general hospital required many people. They were used to ships of less than 500-bed capacity and only limited facilities. The Port officers were agreeably surprised that a long list of repair items had not been thrust at them, very unusual so they said. Answering the operations officer as the sea-duty flag on the jack-staff was being changed to the *Marigold* sponsor's flag, the Captain explained it was always flown in port to honor the Seattle Women's Clubs $4 million effort.

Today, as would happen upon arriving at all the *Marigold*'s principal ports of call, the mail detail was the first ashore. Carrying the outgoing and hurrying back aboard with the incoming mail was the first order of business. For a short time, the letter carriers were the most popular and the two most sought-after men on the ship. Next to home visits, letters from home were the best morale-builders: the familiar making the unfamiliar more bearable, the unpleasant made more pleasant, anxiety eased by reassurance. Letters from home—a magic phrase.

In the afternoon, the Captain made his voyage report to the Superintendent of the Water Division, Colonel Louis Bartoloni, a long-time Army officer and a very versatile one. During the Captain's verbal report, the Colonel listened in on two simultaneous telephone discussions, read three written reports brought in by his aide, signed them, and gave the lieutenant three repair lists to process. The most unusual part of the visit was the Colonel's remembering all the salient points of the voyage report. The Lieutenant later told the Captain he witnessed a scene that went on all day.

When the Port operations officer first boarded the ship, he had told the Captain and the Colonel they would remain in port for ten days. The news spread rapidly and when the hospital staff heard it, they abandoned ship the same afternoon for the Francis Marion Hotel—shore headquarters during the stay in port.

Arrival in Charleston brought the answer to a momentous question that had the staff guessing since leaving Seattle. What did Lieutenant Patricia Carey do with the boxes of the cigars that she bought each week at the ship's store? Had she acquired the habit from the Colonel? Yet nobody had seen her smoke and she deftly parried all probings. But walking down the gangway on her way ashore, it was very evident she carried four separate telltale cigar-box-shaped packages tucked under her arm. The cigars were going to East Grand Forks, Minnesota—her home town.

While the ship's crew and the medics were busy storing and preparing the ship for the oncoming voyage, most of the hospital staff were free to spend their days visiting the historical monuments around Charleston— Fort Sumter, the Powder Magazine, the Citadel Museum, Fort Moultrie and the Old Slave Mart.

Three of the *Portholer* staff, to settle a point, went to St. Michael's Church to take a picture of the exact inscription on the cenotaph in memory of the statesman, Charles C. Pinckney, who was born in Charleston. When he was minister to France in 1789, he made the famous negative reply to France's petition for money because of past favors. The inscription read: "Millions for defense, but not one cent for tribute." The staff hoped it had quoted his true expression, "—not a damned penny for tribute!" It would have had more sock in print.

The city itself, named after King Charles II of England, held great interest for the architecturally minded, as over seventy buildings were pre-Revolutionary and many more dated from the early 18th century. With large fronting balconies, the homes were similar to the New Orleans types, picturesque and charming. For the garden enthusiasts, Charleston's year-round blooming shrubs, trees and flowers were a delight, and the many large public gardens aglow with camellias, azaleas, roses, crepe myrtles and magnolias took up much of the time of the green-thumb group.

Night life for the staff was confined largely to the Francis Marion—the hotel named to honor the famous "Swamp Fox," general of the Revolutionary War. Progressive parties were very popular and, during the cocktail hour, the accounts of the day's activities and ramblings were not as exaggerated as later on, but speculation on the *Marigold's* final destination was still the favorite topic. However, a week's fill of the good life was enough, bringing on a general exodus to the *Marigold* to prepare for the realities of running a hospital.

In the meantime, the Captain had brought aboard the long-awaited news—the *Marigold* was definitely assigned to the Mediterranean Theatre, but specific duty would not be known until arrival in Naples! An indication of what the ship might be doing was the amount of surgical supplies put aboard during the week, which could mean beachhead work. However, a rumor persisted that the ship would end up in England as a base hospital. The resolution was still 4,600 miles away in Italy.

Naples as the ship's destination, having no special significance by itself, was gladly relayed by the personnel to their families and gladly received by them through the many telephone calls that went out all over the country. Ordinarily, relatives were not given exact locations, but were instructed to address overseas mail to APO (Army Post Office) San Francisco or New York.

CHAPTER

III

On July 21st, with the sea-duty flag back on the staff, the *Marigold* passed out of the Cooper River estuary and headed into the Atlantic bound for Napoli and ports unknown. The U.S. Navy routing ended at Rosia Bay, Gibralter, where the British Navy was to provide the Mediterranean route. By sailing the circle course to Cape Spartel in Morocco, 3,600 miles, the run to Gibralter would take thirteen days, unless slowed down by adverse weather. The Navy, in their orders, requested that the *Marigold*'s position, course, and speed be turned in to the radio room every four hours for broadcast on the BAMS schedule, to advise all ships of the presence of a safe-conduct vessel—the Germans monitored all ship broadcasts.

Twice a day for ten days after the weather settled down, two of the doctors gave first aid instructions and demonstrations on the foredeck hatches to groups of the ship's crew. The Captain had asked the Colonel if he would provide lessons in first-aid so the crew would be able to assist in emergencies involving personal injury, should they be called upon. The medics, of course, were well-trained, but the ship's crew, except the officers, had very little knowledge of first aid practices. As a result of the classes, the crew became an integral part of the *Marigold*'s act. And the ship had the distinction of being "Red Cross" in every department.

Except for the three days of rough weather at the outset, the sky remained bright and clear with the surface of the sea reflecting sparkling sunlight and nothing else until 500 miles from Gibralter. Then a shiney oil slick with much debris mixed in appeared, and on the far edge four steel water-logged lifeboats roped together end-to-end wallowed in the light swell. Running in closer, the Captain's 7x50 binoculars showed no evidence of the boats being used—no rowlocks were visible. All the lifeboat equipment was still lashed down including oars, mast and sail. No name or hailing point could be seen. However, other strange circumstances were evident. The line connecting the lifeboats appeared new and unfrayed and the boats were not battered, stove in, or damaged in any way, as would be the case if they had gone through enemy action or been adrift for days. The facts were logged and a notation made that, since there were four lifeboats, they probably came from a passenger vessel.

Also, it was clear from all the ship parts floating around that the *Marigold* was not the first vessel to check on the boats. The oil and debris on the water appeared to be from a sailing ship, one of many brought into war service, carrying a cargo of drum oil, grain and cotton. The surmise proved to be correct when the evidence was reported in Gibralter. The British boarding officer told the Captain the lifeboats were used as a decoy by a submarine towing the boats to different locations and lying in wait for victims, always beyond the area of the Coastal Air Patrol. There may have been a submarine watching the decoys when the *Marigold* passed, but the glasses failed to pick up a periscope within 2,000 yards of the ship. Few seamen would pass up the chance of saving survivors from four lifeboats, in spite of knowing the risk of stopping their ship. The sailing ship, a neutral, went down the day before the *Marigold* passed by and, though equipped with radio, the unfortunate ship was able to get off only name and attack and not location or circumstance. Three days later, using the position given by the *Marigold*, the Royal Navy found and then sank the enemy decoys rather than risk an attack from being slowed down by towing the boats to port.

Arriving at Rosia Bay after clearing the entrance patrol vessel, instructions came out on a high-speed Navy tender to stand by for orders. Backing and filling for three long hours to hold position became a bit galling, especially in view of the advice not to anchor because routing orders would be sent right out. When they did arrive, they were simple—the ship was to proceed to Naples Bay by the safest and most direct route, and there pass into the inner harbor and go alongside the street wharf. Simple, but as it turned out, tricky. The British sub-lieutenant in charge of the tender said they did not know in advance the *Marigold* would be calling at Rosia Bay—hence the delay—a case of one navy not knowing what the other was doing.

Due to the delay at Rosia Bay, a black night enveloped the ship in Gibralter Straits, revealing a maze of floating firepots. Fish nets with warning lights appeared to block every possible route. But after two hours of maneuvering, the long obstacle course was run—no nets were streaming from the bow and no foreign epithets were shouted at the bridge. Dodging nets reminded the Captain of many trips up the Inside Passage to Alaska during the summer salmon runs, swinging hard right and left to avoid tearing up long (1,500 feet) and expensive ($2,000) gill nets, strung from a lantern float to a drift boat.

The last 1,000-mile leg, Gibralter to Naples, would end a voyage of over 10,000 miles from Seattle and bring the *Marigold* into the war zone and into position to show her value and her versatility. The Surgeon General now had a ship in the Mediterranean that could work beach-heads, transport a great number of patients long distances, and provide general hospital services.

In eighty hours steaming, helped with a thirty-knot following wind and passing the southern tip of Sardinia on the way, the whole Gulf of Naples came into view. Another ten miles and then the steep white cliffs of the famed Isle of Capri on the right and Ischia Island on the left, with its ancient stone castle, made everyone realize they were actually in Italy.

To enter the Bay of Naples appeared virtually impossible. Row after row of grey ships of all descriptions were anchored in close order, making an effective barricade. To reach the breakwater entrance leading to the inner harbor would require two miles of maneuvering through a maze of anchored ships. And if the inner harbor turned out to be full, working back out to open water would be a quick aging process. It was clear that with such a large concentration of ships, a major invasion had to be in the making. They had to get through to the dock some way. Undoubtedly the ship was to transport field hospital units to the target area. The Captain quickly decided to head right through between ships to the breakwater entrance leading to the inner harbor and the loading dock.

Enthusiastic yells and whistles coming from the passed ships greeted the *Marigold* nurses lining the promenade deck rails—a touch of feminity for the cooped-up GIs. Sympathy being part of a nurse's character, the girls responded with outstretched arms; even the ship's whistle couldn't have competed with the outburst from the GIs.

About 500 yards from the harbor the binoculars made out two ships anchored close to the breakwater entrance, possibly closing it off. But appearances could be deceiving. The Captain stopped the ship and sent the chief officer in one of the motor lifeboats to see what the chances were. Waiting, the *Marigold* with her twin screws held position without endangering close-by vessels. In thirty minutes, the chief officer was back alongside. Shaking his head, he pointed back down the bay. A ship sunk at the entrance blocked off any angle of approach—damn good thing they were not into that jackpot! Apparently Gibralter didn't subscribe to the Naples papers. The signalling station ashore made no reply to a request for orders and, with darkness not far away, the Captain had no choice but to back out to a turning spot and idle down the gulf until somebody, besides the GIs, acknowledged them. Stern first—with ships close about on both sides and a fifteen-knot wind off the quarter all combined to make the return trip frustrating—turning around or anchoring would be risky with the close formation of ships covering the head of the bay.

Running the GI gauntlet again, the pithy comments to the nurses lining the rails came over loud and clear! "Show a leg—sing us a love song— meet me on Capri—I need a lot of T.L.C.—I've got a heart attack— what's your phone number—come closer, I like perfume!" The banter went on all the way out and at times only 100 feet away. Then the bridge got it. Getting ribbed for taking the girls away didn't make the Captain's job any easier—coping with distractions as well as the ship.

By the time night closed down, the *Marigold* was turned and well clear of the Allied armada. She headed out, not for Rosia Bay, but to cruise up and down the Gulf of Naples at slow speed until morning and then try again to make contact with the British Navy in charge of the port.

At 0800 hours, the *Marigold* reentered the outer harbor and finally received a visual message from a destroyer, relayed from the signal tower, ordering the ship to anchor in a recently vacated position about half a mile from the harbor wall. The chart showed forty-five fathoms, rather deep for anchoring in an exposed area. However, the *Marigold* had ample anchor chain; each chain locker housed ten shots, 900 feet. Even so, the usual practice of three fathoms of chain to each fathom of depth wasn't possible with neighboring ships close aboard, restricting swinging room. But calm weather would eliminate the danger of dragging and the forecast was favorable. With the anchor down and after sixteen days at sea, the engines were silent. The *Marigold* had now joined the 700 ships waiting for the big push.

However, the Captain and the Colonel didn't intend to mark time; they were ready to go ashore and find out what was planned for them, but two lieutenant colonels, aides to the port surgeon, saved them the trip. After a welcome aboard, they were ushered to the lounge and immediately apologized for yesterday's lack of communiction, due to the office-force being in the field. Then they began right in answering the question, "Where do we go from here?"

"Here's the whole story, for your ears only." The completeness of the planned offensive amazed the Captain and Colonel; they didn't miss a word. Southern France would be invaded in a matter of days; the invasion was termed "Operation Anvil." The purpose was fourfold: relieve pressure on Eisenhower's armies in Normandy; open the Rhone Valley for a drive on Paris; eliminate the U-boat and the Luftwaffe menace in the western Mediterranean; and take Toulon for a naval base and Marseilles for a shipping port. Seventh Army troops would hit the Riviera beaches on D-Day; then the following day the French Expeditionary Corps would join the assault. The invasion fleet, staged at Naples and Corsican ports, was an Allied force, with the U.S. providing 515 vessels, Britain 273, France 12, Greece 7. The invasion force had over 1,300 landing craft available and the naval support force had 83 destroyers, several heavy ships and carriers. Corsica had been seized by the free French in 1943 and the airfields were now in use as bases for the air support forces. All the elements for success were present. The striking forces poised. Liberation of Southern France was assured.

The *Marigold's* part would be to treat casualties at the beachheads and then evacuate them to Naples. The exact locations on the coast would not be given until departure day, the day following the landings. "There, you have it all. We're very glad to have a ship like this in the Mediterranean; you can do about anything for us. Now we should see your hospital; Colonel Rudolph, the port surgeon, is especially interested in your upper-deck wards. You might have field nurses to take along to the beachheads."

They had also said there would be a wait of several days and, as it turned out, seven anxious days would come and go before the fleet of ships with their troops, guns, vehicles, tanks and supplies moved out. To keep active, the staff and crew used the respite to shop, walk and jeep around Naples, Pompei, Sorrento, and the bold ones even talked their way to Rome. The stay-aboards in the meantime came up with a rewarding project. Since the troops on transports were not allowed ashore, and to provide a little diversion for the GIs, eight—sometimes more—of the personnel cruised around the transports in the motorboat, exchanging hails and barbs. The troops always blew kisses to the nurses as a parting salute—kudos for giving them a lift.

Shopping in Naples stores was more than just a pastime. Finely made metal jewelry, filigree work with gemstones, kid gloves, lace of all descriptions, and most anything of a decorative nature was obtainable. The prices were reasonable and the *Marigold* shoppers loaded up. The only real deterrent to their absorbing shopping was the ever-present rank odor and the street filth, but with a war going on there were no complaints.

The favorite attraction for the music lovers was attending the San Carlo Opera Theatre matinees, no night liberty permitted, to be thrilled by the singing of Rigoletto, Aida, Il Trovotore and all the well-known operas. The costumes were a bit worn and the opera house in need of refurbishing, but the singers more than made up for the dinginess. The theatre was filled at all performances and almost entirely with soldiers from the Mediterranean campaigns; all the Allied nations were represented. The dramatic singing was a great reliever of war tension. The expression "Music is good for the soul" proved out at the San Carlo Opera House.

The *Marigold*'s romance-minded were offered a trip to the Isle of Capri and twenty-five responded to the Captain's invitation. They spent the afternoon visiting San Michele—the old Roman villa beautifully rebuilt by Axel Munthe and described in his book, *San Michele*. The Funicular Railroad, Anacapri (top of Capri), and the Blue Grotto, open to the sea, were all visited. The quality wine of the island, Lacrima Christi, was frequently sampled to honor the name. Time ran out long before the wine and as the entire Naples area would be blacked out at night and the ship an hour away, the trip had to end, but the Isle of Capri, the pearl of the sea, would long be remembered by the fortunate twenty-five.

Every night during the first hours of blackout, German planes came over to keep informed of any large ship movement. The reconnaissance planes flew at a high altitude, dropping star shells, lighting up the entire harbor so they could count the ships. Powerful long-range searchlights picked out the planes flying above the floating lights and anti-aircraft guns pumped away at the intruders—occasionally Jerry didn't get back home. On the *Marigold*, orders were to stay under cover. Shrapnel from the bursts rained on the steel deck with a clink like a duck hit in a shooting gallery. With all the fire power aboard the hundreds of ships in the harbor, the Luftwaffe apparently decided the odds were too great to risk planes on frequent bombing attacks. It would be easier to catch the ships when they were underway or at the beaches.

Three more U.S. Army hospital ships arrived, the *Thistle* and *Arcadia*, former small Atlantic coast passenger vessels, and the larger *Emily Weeder*, named for a nurse killed in the war. Comparing the four ships, the *Marigold*'s lines and structure were more impressive. She looked more comfortable and the unified appearance more satisfying to the eye—at least that was the Captain's opinion. The Army had two more hospital ships, built up on Liberty-ship hulls, that hadn't put in an appearance—the *Jasmine* and the *Wisteria*. Whoever gave the ships floral names must have been a former horticulturist.

To bear out the Captain's private surmise that the ship would soon be underway and headed for the target area, several units of field hospital nurses from the 7th Army were assigned to the *Marigold* for transportation to the beachheads. The veteran nurses were cared for with great regard; they were given every consideration to make their days before landing as pleasant as possible. The result was a commendatory letter from Major General Stayer and Major General Larkin, with many endorsements, sent to the *Marigold* staff—a high compliment for their efforts in behalf of the nurses.

Regardless of the varied diversions, the pre-departure tension continued to build up. It was all-pervasive. But on August 14, 1944 it broke: Tomorrow was D-Day. With mixed emotions, the *Marigold* people watched ship after ship pull out for the combat zone. The next time they would meet, the surroundings would not be so protected. Just watching the transports and destroyers get under way, waiting for their own turn, was hard to take. However, knowing that tasks would come up that only the *Marigold* could handle made the waiting to get going more bearable.

CHAPTER

IV

The *Marigold*'s turn came August 16th. That day the British Naval Office called the Captain ashore to discuss the routing to the target area. Before leaving, he told the engineers to warm up the engines, and the chief officer was to make sure everyone was present and accounted for. All the way back to the ship in the motorboat, the Captain mulled over the Navy's information and route until they were well fixed in his mind. Coming alongside and looking up at the main deck, he thought everyone on the ship must be at the rail. Back aboard, he quickly explained that the *Marigold* was to head for the Straits of Bonifacio, between Corsica and Sardinia, then on to St. Maxime in the Gulf of Tropez, along the south coast of France. The *Marigold* was to stand by off the St. Maxime beaches and take aboard casualties as they developed. Invasion landings had been made at the French Riviera ports of St. Tropez, St. Maxime, Frejus, St. Raphael and Cannes, but St. Maxime was the main thrust, the *Marigold*'s area. They were on their way. Suddenly the months of preparation were to become months of active service. From now on every move was for real.

Northbound, all the heavy traffic encountered traveled in convoys, and several of the unloaded transports and supply ships showed blackened and torn plates—evidence the action had started. The flood of ships didn't ease up before making Bonifacio Straits and, as the Captain had pre-planned, they made a daylight run through the congested straits—clearing heavy traffic and sunken ships would have been difficult at night. Even in the open forty-five-mile stretch south of Cape Ferro, dangers were present; ten ships had been sunk, causing hazards day or night.

From the west entrance of the straits at Cape Testa, the course held to a straight line for St. Maxime, a night run of 170 miles to the northwest. Running in the dark without a moon or radar, clearing groups of blacked-out ships, had the Captain and the bridge watch constantly searching ahead, trying to locate them in time to maneuver. Thankfully, the destroyer-escort vessels riding herd on the convoys were a great help by signalling with their blue spotlights the position of vessels and the location of clear lanes. When dawn broke on the day of arrival, the engine's turns were increased to make up for the time lost during the night. The Captain again planned for an early daytime arrival at St. Maxime so casualties could be loaded quickly and safely during daylight hours.

The thud of heavy gunfire rolled down to the ship from ten miles away and increased in intensity as the beach area came into view. At a mile from shore, a visual signal came from the Navy communications ship, a forest of antennas and scanners sprouting from the superstructure. The *Marigold* was to anchor close to "Yellow Beach" and begin loading from LCVPs (landing craft vehicle personnel) coming alongside. With the small, low-to-the-water boats, the ship's gear would have to be used to lift the patients to the deck. The Navy beachmaster came aboard and spotted the ship only 300 yards from shore; that decided the Captain to hold position with the engines. He informed the Captain that, if the German's usual plan continued, no bombing would occur until dusk—and then look out! But the enemy guns located on the distant, red-colored hills above the beach would be firing continuously all day long—the shells exploding all over the harbor area. The close guns had been silenced by naval gunfire, and support bombing had made it possible for the troops to overrun the German positions. He also said thousands of paratroopers were dropped inland to seal off the highways and supply line and, since they met with little opposition, they had the German troops completely isolated in the coastal area. Suddenly the beachmaster stopped talking, pointed towards the shore, and said, "There's two boatloads on the way," and he hurried down the deck ladder to spot the LCVPs.

In minutes, the two bow-ramp boats came alongside and made fast opposite number two and three hatches. The ship's loading booms (derricks) were already positioned, and the shallow, open-top litter boxes hooked on the winch falls. Slots halfway down the ends of the box held the handles in place and the litters off the bottom. Some of the litters were metal Stokes baskets, indicating the casualties were from ships, but ninety percent were the canvas and pole type. Litters completely covered the flat, unobstructed bottom of the boats. The *Marigold's* winch drivers were practiced and very careful with the levers, and the chief officer directing the loading at the rail kept a close watch on the litters every foot of the way up. The boxes landed on mattress cushions, and teams of medical attendants quickly lifted and carried the litters along the main deck a short distance to the doorway leading into the hospital area. One of

Shell bursts (flak) of the type experienced by the *MARIGOLD* in the Mediterranean and South Pacific. (U.S. Coast Guard photo)

USAHS *MARIGOLD* enroute to Seattle after commissioning in June 1944. (Joe Williamson photo)

Commissioning ceremony at the Tacoma shipyard June 10, 1944. The ships complement is on the main deck. The commissioning officers are on the boat deck. Note the name of the navy transport ship in the upper left of the photo has been blanked out to prevent the vessel's identification during wartime. (U.S. Army Signal Corps photo)

the doctors stationed at the entrance scanned the patients' medical tags and directed the litter bearers to the proper ward. Empty litters went back ashore with the boats. During the time loading was going on, the Captain stood on the bridge wing, keeping close watch on the foredeck, the boats, the harbor, and the sky.

All the casualties had received first aid and many had been given some preliminary treatment in the field hospitals, so their bandages were clean and white. The majority of the men suffered from gunshot, shrapnel and fragmentation wounds. Three hundred of the patients were ambulatory and there were several mental cases accompanied by escorts. With very little time for recovery, all the wounded showed the strain of pain on their faces, yet attempted smiles when they saw the *Marigold's* sheltering surroundings.

Many of the wounded were from Africa—Ghoums, Senegalese and Arabs (French expeditionary soldiers) wearing earrings and faces showing tribal markings. They weren't in the fight for the money; their reason was the same as the GI's. But they fought differently; they were night fighters, penetrating enemy lines by stealth and with long knives dispatching the unwary. Some of the native French Colonials carried a little pouch attached to their wrist containing German ears—the same idea as scalping practiced by the American Indians in the pioneering days. However, for sanitary reasons, before reaching Naples it became necessay for the ward nurses, Lucille Lennart and Helen Shuster, to dispose of the pouches. It was harrowing work, not knowing the dialect, to try calming fighters reluctant to give up their spoils. The girls said that, unconsciously, whenever they were near the beds of the Ghoums, both hands went up to their ears.

Loading continued non-stop for three hours until six hundred patients were aboard, completely clearing out the beach hospital and first-aid stations. But the ship was asked to stand by until afternoon when more casualties would be coming from the front. In the meantime, an LST (landing ship tank) would come alongside and take off the 7th Army nurses, bag and baggage. Not knowing how late in the day the ship would have to wait, the Captain moved two miles out from the beach to a safer location, the LST following along to debark the nurses—many of them bronze-star veterans. The girls had planned a special *au revoir* for the time when they had to leave and, due to the LST's high deck, a short gangplank from the *Marigold's* side port to the LST gave the nurses a level walkway for their performance. As they slowly left the ship, the beautiful, stirring melody of the *Marseillaise*, coming from sixty pleasant voices permeating both ships, brought everybody able to walk out on deck. The nurses finished the anthem from the LST's deck and the applause sounded like the San Carlo Opera audience calling for an encore. As a serenade to the *Marigold*, it was tremendous—march on!

In mid-afternoon the recall came, and after shifting back to the beach the boats brought out fifty more litters. Then word came that the number of wounded brought to the field hospitals was decreasing, so the ship was to leave for Naples, there to discharge the patients and return to the target area.

As the weatherman remembered his obligation to the patients, the sea remained calm for their comfort and the medical staff accomplished their work without coping with rock and roll. Tennie Oetken, one of the surgical nurses, said their team worked so much faster with the ship level! And another surgical nurse, Mae Griep, added that, with so much suturing for the surgeons to do, having both hands free to work was a godsend.

However, for the deck officers the first night out was not so favorable. The weather, though calm, turned misty and black with poor visibility— although no problems developed until reaching Boniface Straits. Then, due to the straits being restricted at the eastern end by several islands blocking parts of the entrance, the passage suddenly became compli- cated—and not just from rocks and shoals.

About three in the morning a blue signal light flashed off the port beam and the *Marigold* signalman standing by on the bridge called out the code message as it came in: "You are into an eighty-ship convoy; proceed dead slow; hold straight course; will advise." A "Wilco" went back to the destroyer. Fifteen minutes later the bridge watch relaxed; the destroyer with its seeing-eye radar came back with an all-clear signal. The Captain asked for a route around the convoy and the destroyer requested the ship's speed, then replied, "Follow my blue light." In thirty minutes the convoy was astern, the destroyer thanked, and with the sky getting lighter, the Captain's sixth cup of coffee was sipped in leisure.

All the way south the Chaplains spent endless hours listening to the patients' problems, mistakes, hopes and illusions. Naturally, the Chap- lains' treatment was more spiritual than physical, but effective. Their axiom seemed to be, "Where there was a will, there was a way." To strengthen the will was their objective. Their ministry was vital to the healing process, instilling confidence and hope—being compassionate, not sentimental.

Coming into Naples Bay this time, August 21st, presented no piloting problems with only the back-up ships swinging at anchor. By blinker, orders came to debark the patients to ambulances over the deck of a German hospital ship hull berthed next to the concrete bulkhead at the marina. Surprised, the Captain asked for the repeat of the ironic message.

The reply was the same, so he headed for the unusual berth, still wondering if the wording was totally correct.

It was, and the *Marigold* berthed alongside the rusty hulk. Ambulance after army ambulance pulled up, were quickly loaded and moved on to the base hospital. Six hours and the *Marigold*'s wards were empty, the goodbyes and godspeeds only echoes.

Going ashore in Naples was now a simple matter. Collecting cameos and intaglios turned out to be the special interest during the lay-over in port. Beautifully carved flowers, Roman heads and initials in pink, green and black in rings, pins and bracelets were all highly prized by their finders. But, as before, the excitement of shopping couldn't compete with the singing at the San Carlo Opera; it remained the favorite afternoon entertainment.

With a three-day wait for sailing orders, ways and means were considered to improve the *Marigold*'s service by analyzing the first effort. However, the staff didn't lose a patient, and the medical care proved to be just what the doctor ordered. The hospital had functioned admirably as programmed. No ship malfunctions occurred, thanks to the engineers. The trip had progressed safely and timely, and the loading of patients couldn't have gone better. With the results all positive, the *Marigold*'s fitness for the job was very evident. The hospital complement and crew could now be more confident, knowing they had a smooth-functioning ship, and for their part they knew the job would always be "well done."

A return to St. Maxime was expected, but orders came for St. Tropez, with departure scheduled for August 24th. This time the routing office gave the Captain a route well clear of the convoy lanes. The course looked safe and easy except for the initial leg which ran right through the island of Ischia! Being of a practical turn of mind, the Captain figured he could save time by going around the island and coming back to the course on the other side, even if the shortest distance between two points was a straight line.

At the briefing session, the Navy was proud to relate that the German submarine menace was lessening due to their lack of supply bases in the Mediterranean. The British Navy had clobbered them. Even the picket boats at Gibralter hadn't heard a submarine ping with their sonar for some time. But the Navy was not proud to relate that the German bombers were still raining destruction on land and sea.

Upon arrival in the morning off St. Tropez, word came by signal searchlight from the Navy control vessel to come close in-shore at the head of the bay two miles from the town. The message came from SOPA, senior officer present afloat, since the U.S. Navy conducted amphibious operations, and all shore-side activity came under its jurisdiction—including patient evacuation from the beaches.

The Navy beachmaster, a lieutenant, came aboard and informed the Captain there had been a severe air raid the night before and the *Marigold*'s arrival was a blessing. There were many casualties to bring aboard as soon as possible—the field hospital was overflowing. The lieutenant also told the Captain that the German guns on the hill were still raising hell and the ship might have to move out in a hurry. To confirm the warning, four shells in quick succession exploded, straddling the *Marigold*; a destroyer astern was no doubt the target. Before the concussions rolled away and the water geysers subsided, the Captain had slammed the engine telegraph to FULL AHEAD. He didn't sound the general alarm to prevent undue confusion—in a few minutes the ship would be in the clear. Fortunately, he had not anchored after sensing the danger of the confined and crowded area. While the Lieutenant—apparently used to having shells following him around—continued talking, the ship forged ahead up the bay, away from the anchored navy ships. "That was the closest one today; that battery now will be spotted by the fly boys." The Lieutenant looked at the sky and said that Jerry came over every day at dusk and dropped eggs more or less hit and miss. After the remark, there wasn't any question—the Captain wouldn't anchor and the engines would remain on standby.

The Lieutenant stayed on the bridge and, while waiting for the casualties to start arriving, told the Captain the Germans had become very active in the Gulf of Tropez, with corvetts and torpedo boats. They had damaged several Allied vessels and sunk two. In one engagement, two German corvetts attacked two British corvetts, inflicting severe damage, but the British boats, under command of Douglas Fairbanks, Jr., didn't give up; they eventually sank the enemy boats.

The Lieutenant also alerted the Captain to watch out for German fanatics riding torpedoes and small boats, loaded with 500 pounds of explosives, steering them all the way to a ship's side. They were suicide runs and deadly. The human torpedoes, eighteen feet long, could submerge to 100 feet in traveling under water, making them hard to spot. The Captain quickly commented that it all sounded like the Germans were desperate. He asked if it was true the 7th Army had advanced inland to the Rhone Valley and that the entire German 19th Army (100,000 men) was in retreat. The Lieutenant didn't know, but he did hear that the French Division had captured Toulon, Marseilles and, with it, 50,000 German troops. But on the *Marigold*'s next trip the Lieutenant expected to have a run-down on how General Truscott and his army were doing up the Rhone Valley.

After watching an LSM (landing ship medium) with the first load of casualties ease alongside, the Captain turned his attention to the foredeck, and the Lieutenant with a quick handshake went below to give orders to the LSM where to pick up the next load. The LSM's deck being too low for a gangplank, the ship's gear went into action and the litters came aboard as fast as the winch could safely bring them up. Not only was dispatch important to get the wounded into the hospital but, with the LSMs, only one set of ship's gear could be used—lengthening the loading time—and the captain wanted all the casualties aboard by dark.

The loading continued until late in the afternoon, close to the time of Jerry's daily visit; then, a half hour before the last LSM pulled away, an LST with 400 troops aboard passed by, headed for the beach to unload. Troop debarking had just started when the German guns found the range and shelled the LST, inflicting horrendous damage to both men and ship. SOPA signalled to come in and stand by to take the casualties as fast as the first-aid stations released them. And in an hour they started to arrive alongside, their bandages more red than white. The *Marigold*'s surgical teams were prepared and they worked non-stop until every wound was treated. In World War I, Dakins Solution and Iodoform were the simple antiseptics for dressing wounds but now, fortunately, antibiotics were working wonders in the *Marigold*'s wards, preventing infection, saving lives.

Before all the litters reached the *Marigold*, the bombers came over and started their nightly destruction. They plastered the beaches first, but it was only a matter of time before the harbor would get it. At the first explosion, the Captain signalled SOPA on the ship's vulnerability. "Seven hundred patients aboard; imperative to shift out of harbor." SOPA agreed, but advised of one more load of casualties aboard an LSM. The Captain replied he would go at slow speed and for the LSM to follow and catch up.

A half mile from the harbor the LSM came alongside and made fast, fenders absorbing the slight surge. Eighty-eight patients were hoisted aboard in thirty-three minutes—a remarkable feat using only one set of gear. All the casualties from the shelled LST were now safely aboard and in good hands.

After giving the crew of the LSM a carton stuffed with candy, fruit, and cakes, the tie-up lines were dropped, and the *Marigold*'s engines turned up to full bore for Naples. In ten hours, the ship had loaded 776 patients, eleven over normal capacity. The preponderance of patients were American, with two hundred Free French, Indo-Chinese, Foreign Legionnaires, Moroccans and Zouaves, and twenty wounded German POWs under guard. Two of the prisoners had German flags in their kits. These were promptly weighted and sunk. The Colonel and all hands agreed the Nazi's black swastika reminded them of the poisonous black widow spider.

The St. Tropez patients were generally in more serious condition than those from St. Maxime, particularly the shelled LST casualties. The staff worked unceasingly, applying all that medical science had to offer to save every life; but, even so, four succumbed on the way south. They became martyrs to the cause and they surely would receive a martyr's reward.

With the invasion now two weeks along, mental breakdowns had started to occur, and St. Tropez put aboard fifty cases of psychoneurosis, dementia praecox and acute psychosis. Captain Ross, the psychiatrist, described the disorders as induced by anxiety. None of the patients were aggressive so the neuropsychopathic wards were quiet, but to make sure, they were confined in the wards for the short trip. Captain Ross said sedation was given to help them rest and, in some cases, sodium amatol administered to bring out and talk out the problems causing the mental disturbance. In most anxiety cases, he was able to restore balance by the simple treatment.

Ambulatory patients were allowed on deck and dressed in medical corps gray pajamas and red robes; they looked and appeared anything but soldiers fresh from the front. The complete change of environment acted like a quick tonic, and smiles replaced the gaunt lost look when they came aboard.

Early in the morning, orders came by radio to call at Ajaccio in Corsica to pick up ten patients. With the port close to the track, the ship was in the roadstead at 0900 hours. Signalling started and shortly an LSM came alongside with the injured, all native French Colonials and mostly fracture cases, resulting from jeep accidents. Fortunately they required very little attention, as communication with them was a problem. Having so many different languages and dialects to contend with, the medical corps should have had a foreign language school so the nurses could say, "Turn on your side" in more than one language.

By making up the time lost at Ajaccio, the *Marigold* was fast alongside her former berth in time to discharge the patients on the day of arrival. In a demonstration of team work, the ship's medical attendants acting as litter bearers, in a record time of two hours, completely emptied the wards. The medics didn't expect compliments, but they came to them anyway.

Since the *Marigold* was ordered to remain alongside, and no subsequent orders came to anchor in the Bay, the inference was that the Naples Base hospital and not the Riviera beaches would be loading the ship. For five days no enlightenment came from the port surgeon's office and, as the crew had little desire to further explore Naples, the ship was given a thorough cleaning inside and out, including all the Red Cross markings.

Captain Mieczkowski was the only one of the staff who had a serious interest ashore. He hoped the ship would be in Naples on September 19th because that was the feast day of St. Januarius, patron saint of Naples, whose solidified blood in a vial would miraculously liquify on September 19th. The miracle had a 400-year history, and the Father wanted to witness the event at Naples Cathedral. Unfortunately for the Chaplain, sailing orders came on September 4th. However, he wasn't disappointed in his quest for more of the Camillian red crosses. The 100 he had placed in the chapel, inside leaflets, were all taken. This time, there would be two hundred of the felt cloth crosses, with pins attached, ready for the patients—most of whom pinned the small red crosses on their bandages rather than on their pajama tops, evidence they hadn't considered them just a decoration.

As generally surmised, the port surgeon's orders, through the Navy office, were not for returning to France. Instead, they instructed the ship to take a full load of patients to Charleston—loading and sailing September 5th! The sudden change of destination confirmed the thinking that the casualty rate was continuing to decrease and the invasion forces were encountering less and less resistance. For the *Marigold*, this sign of victory would mean a change in service. Instead of Naples to the Riviera, it would be Naples to Charleston—a liner hospital ship.

CHAPTER

V

So, on September 5th, a steady stream of army ambulances from the Base hospital delivered a full load of patients to the *Marigold* in six hours, largely casualties from the African campaign. And as scheduled, on September 5th, with the personnel not a bit unhappy to be returning to the States, the ship left a depressing Naples for a buoyant Charleston. Nevertheless, to the staff, the realities of Hitler's war and the cost of freedom so evident in the wards of the *Marigold* would remain in their minds—payment for that pearl of great price.

The Mediterranean passage turned out pleasant all the way and, for the Captain's peace of mind, the ship was not routed via Rosia Bay for ongoing orders. But approaching Gibralter, as in August, the fishermen were out in force with their fire pots bobbing as a warning to stay clear of the nets. With the Straits of Gibralter fourteen kilometers wide, the fishermen still set up in the traffic lanes. However, one generous family made up for the interference by coming alongside and sending up a large tub of fish, the size and appearance of carp. They ended up on the dinner trays of the medical attendants. Fried in olive oil according to instructions from the fisherman, the fish were described as *delicioso*.

Abeam of Cape Spartel the course changed to head on the first segment of the circle course, the shortest distance to Charleston. Passing into the Atlantic, the sea still favored the patients; only a low swell disturbed the surface. But in another month the mild weather would start to deteriorate, leading to strong northerlies and violent winter storms. Then the *Marigold* would have to light more joss sticks to the weatherman.

The eighty-degree warm weather was salubrious, but the sudden increase to ninety, with the smoke going straight up, was uncomfortable, especially below decks. Due to the hot weather, the *Marigold* was using twenty gallons of water per man per day, approximately 24,000 gallons in twenty-four hours. In the sailing ship days, two quarts per man per day was allowed and one quart of a man's ration went to the cook. In the *Marigold's* case, a percentage of the twenty gallons went not only for cooking and personal use but to the ship's laundry. In a year's time the laundry washed over 100,000 sheets and 120,000 towels, and no salt water was used. Without the evaporators making 100 tons of fresh water from salt water every day, the staff would have to operate Chinese hand-laundry style.

Strange as it may seem, when two days out and when crossing the same latitude and longitude where the sailing ship disappeared by torpedo or gunfire, another oil slick a mile long appeared. With the black oil still thick and only a small area of spread, whatever occurred had to be recent. It was not a case of a ship pumping out bilges; the color was wrong.

From the flying bridge, a smudge on the horizon dead ahead could be made out. As the distance closed and, encountering more patches of oil, a ship took form, apparently moving at a slow speed. Coming up on the vessel's port beam, but holding off a half mile, the cause of the oil spill was explained. From the bow of number two hatch on the near side, hull plates, deck plates, frames and beams were torn apart and jutting out at all angles, forming gaping holes all along the side from the main deck to below the water line.

The ship turned out to be a fast Australian refrigerated carrier with the name painted out so no identification could be made in port or at sea. The ship responded by blinker that they had been outbound light, struck a detached mine during the night, and were forced to head for the States and drydock. They were under control and would be joined by an escort in twelve hours.

The Captain held back the true facts from the ship's company, explaining the damaged ship had been in collision, which was true enough. He knew that the results of hitting a floating mine, with the visual evidence close at hand, would upset the *Marigold's* handicapped patients. As he intended, the damaged ship created only an undisturbing topic of conversation.

Ever since leaving Naples, extra lookouts had been posted during the night as an added precaution. The reefer ship was a potent reminder that the hours of darkness held the greatest danger. However, except along coasts, the chances of striking a mine were not great, but with ocean winds and currents carrying them along, they covered a wide area, making the danger ever-present.

Halfway across, the ship's peaceful routine was broken by a piercing cry of "Man overboard." Spotting a bobbing head in the water, the bridge watch swung the ship hard left away from the man, threw over a life ring and, with the Captain quickly on the bridge, one engine was reversed to help head the ship toward the man. The senior watch officer, Roy Robeck, on the flying bridge with binoculars, was able to keep the black head in sight. But in another minute he yelled, "No sign of the man." Roy said he couldn't see any attempt by the patient to save himself. The area was well searched using one of the motor lifeboats and, regrettably, the boat returned with an empty life ring. The entry in the logbook stated that a group of mental patients had been taken up on the afterdeck to enjoy the sun, breeze and companionship. Six attendnts were on hand. Even so, the disturbed patient—not uttering a sound—suddenly broke for the rail and leaped overboard. The case was classed "psychoneurosis, anxiety state."

The sad event lowered the spirits of witnesses to the tragedy and they went about their work with greater intensity. The neuropsychopathic wards were exremely hot, and relief on the deck had to continue but, to minimize the risk, group size was cut and time on deck reduced. But more frequent visits were allowed. All patients were required to remain seated. As an aid in spotting any future jumpers, the Captain had orange smoke cannisters placed in the bridge wings with orders to throw one overboard with the life ring as soon as a cry was heard.

It was not long in coming. Again, in the afternoon of the next day, a shouted "Man overboard" came from the afterdeck and, a few seconds later, "Man overboard" came from amidships! Two smoke floats hit the water, belching fountains of orange smoke. Then, according to plan, the engines were put at full astern and, while the ship was coming to a stop, the motorboat was lowered close to the water. With the way off and engines stopped, the motorboat dropped to the water and was away for the floats. With the chief officer at the tiller, the boat made a straight course for a raised arm. Coming alongside, the crew pulled the man aboard, apparently the second jumper. The boat then circled the area, looking for the first man, and the *Marigold* came up to join in. After an hour of cruising the area, the search was abandoned.

The second man, an infantry captain and a patient suffering from battle fatigue, saw the first man jump and dived in hoping to assist him. The soldier captain said he could see the fellow and started swimming toward him but he suddenly disappeared and never came up. From what he could see, this man, like the previous one, made no attempt to survive or swim to the life ring. (The cork rings were designed to support twenty pounds over and above the body's own floating capability.) Captain Ross listed the suicide as "psychoneurosis, constitutional state."

Providentially or not, no more attempts were made to satisfy the uncontrollable urge to find peace in the silvery, shimmering, sun-filled ocean. Attendants standing right at the rail were ready to exercise complete control of any untoward move. Peace and quiet again reigned, and only occasional radio programs or announcements, coming from the public-address system, broke in on the lulling sounds of water brushing the ship's side. The patients had asked for just rest and relaxation and, with many of them bed-ridden, the planned entertainments were not held.

When the ship came to the latitude of the Charleston entrance radio beacon, the course was set at due west and, at fifty miles off, direction-finder bearings were started and the beam followed the rest of the way in. Speed was reduced to pass the sea-buoy at daylight and pick up a pilot for the run up the river to the Army base. The ETA Charleston, September 22nd, was easily made, with the weather cooperating all the way.

This time, a string of ambulances was the reception committee, and immediately the tie-up lines were made fast; two gangways were lifted into the side ports and discharging began, ambulatory patients first. By 1400 hours the ship was cleared of patients, clean-up finished, and everyone not on duty free to leave. Some of the medics obtained only short leave and others had enough time to visit at home. Before the abandon-ship took place, General Kirk, Surgeon General of the Army, his staff, and General Duke, Port Commander, paid a visit to the ship and complimented the personnel on their record and the spruce conditions throughout. Words of priase from the top General gave the staff a feeling of accomplishment and confidence. It was good medicine.

The Captain was informed the layover in port would be short as the ship was scheduled to depart for Oran, Algeria and provide service from there to Naples and on to the States. The new run more or less agreed with the consensus of opinion arrived at before leaving Naples. But the Army didn't always follow the process of deduction.

Continued operation out of Charleston caused consternation to many of the ship's crew from Seattle. Discussing the situation with the Captain, they said for the long term they preferred to sail out of the Seattle Port of Embarkation. Many of them had spent much of their seafaring days on the Alaska runs, more familiar territory, cooler and of course allowing regular visits at home. It wasn't that they wouldn't make a sacrifice for the good of the ship, but as long as all ships had to be manned then why not Charleston crews for Charleston ships and Seattle crews for Seattle ships? Of course their reasoning was only an assumption, as all crews and all men were not equal in ability or experience. Nevertheless, they had a point but the loss of able and knowledgeable men was bound to be felt. They had been specially selected. The break-up of a tried crew and filling in with untried crewmen would be a serious impediment where *esprit de corps* was essential for success. The Captain, justifiably annoyed with the unexpected development, nevertheless discussed the requests for transfer to Seattle with the Manning Division, and they also reluctantly agreed, provided the men remained until replacements could be obtained. This was accomplished and, in five days, all the engineers, chief steward, chief officer, two watch officers, some of the petty officers, seamen, and black gang were authorized to leave for Seattle.

As the Captain anticipated, crew replacements were a problem due to the large number of ships sailing out of Charleston; seamen were scarce, and those with experience had long since been placed. The *Marigold* required seasoned and well-balanced types, so only a few of the replacements qualified. However, to the Captain's satisfaction, the second officer, Roy Robeck, two junior officers, and many of the petty officers and deck department seamen stayed with the ship. The Filipinos, competent and dependable, remained. Charleston provided a chief and third officer. Fortunately, the other deck officer vacancies could be filled by promotions. Rex Harwood, junior officer, advanced to third officer, replacing Ray Fosse who was returning to navigation school. Fred Mathews was promoted from quartermaster to junior officer and quartermaster Donald McKay replaced John Hogan as junior officer. Dick Richings remained with the ship as junior officer. The new steward and the new engineers were all Charleston men. Only time would reveal the effect of the turnover; it had been a case of Hobson's choice—none at all.

CHAPTER

VI

T wo days before the intended departure for Oran, Colonel Bartoloni called the Captain in about an unusual opportunity for the *Marigold*. The Colonel went right to the point. An Army hospital ship was needed for the South Pacific and what about the *Marigold* going? The ship would be assigned to the Los Angeles Port of Embarkation, but she might never see Los Angeles. Was the *Marigold* equipped to work in the South Pacific for long periods? The Captain's answer was affirmative, except that more forced ventilation and some lesser items should be provided. The Colonel looked pleased, and agreed to do as much work as possible and yet meet the October 9th departure date. That would give only twelve days to outfit for an indefinite stay in an area where supply and maintenance were problems. The Colonel pointed to a plaque in his office with the Santayana boast, "The difficult we do immediately, the impossible may take a little longer." This would have to come true if the *Marigold* was to be ready by October 9th.

When the Captain told the medical staff of the change in direction, they were surprised, but not dismayed, after all the only change would be environment. From pine trees to palm trees, from Germans to Japanese, from low humidity to high humidity—a matter of adjustment, though a radical one. The staff now would have to obtain complete hospital supplies for a year and do the same for themselves, books heading the list.

To be close to the source of supply of all categories, the Francis Marion Hotel again became the uptown headquarters and all shopping and shore activity originated and ended there. Room visiting and exchanging hospitality would again be the principal indoor recreation. Living ashore had a seldom-considered benefit. After weeks of looking out of the ship's small round portholes, the hotel's large square windows cured any tendency to cabin claustrophobia.

During the stay in port, Captain Beebe and Captain Smoloroff became majors and many of the medics received higher ratings. But the hard-working nurses remained lieutenants. Promotion to captain wouldn't occur until taking charge of a unit similar to the *Marigold* group. The comments aboard were that the Army should have at least raised their pay for South Pacific duty.

Two days before sailing everyone reported aboard and ready for the five week voyage. Not so the Captain, he had another item to rustle up. He had asked the Navy Yard if they could provide the ship with a range-finder. Anchoring instructions at beachheads were given in so many yards from a designated ship or object, so acquiring a rangefinder, giving distance away in yards, would simplify spotting the ship in an assigned position. Mounted on a pedestal on the flying bridge, the instrument would have a 360° sweep and when not in use it would be adequately covered so not to be mistaken as a gunfire control device. The Navy Yard came through, they loaned the ship, a used two meter coincidence type. Fortunately it was not a stereoscopic rangefinder, which for accurate reading required an operator with double vision. The Army Maintenance and Repair Department did their part, they fabri-cated and installed the mount and the Captain was pleased with the result. But he had one far-reaching disappointment, no reliable charts of the South Pacific were available. With miles of coral reefs to contend with and not knowing their exact location, trial and error piloting, with no margin for error, would prove a rather perilous undertaking. Maybe Panama could supply useable charts.

The Port completed most of the asked-for work and filled the want-list except the request for a high speed shoreboat—they were all stocked in California. However, the most important item and concern could be crossed off. The new axial-flow blowers now circulated more air and faster and particularly relieved the stifling heat in the Neuropsychopathic wards. Lieutenant Carey, the charge-nurse, said she lost fifteen pounds on the Naples trip from the high temperature below decks. Due to the heat she and her assistants were solely tried keeping the mental patients under control. It was not too difficult under normal conditions, but in a hotbox they became unruly and the medics had to cope with physical attacks. Lieutenant Carey sent a letter of thanks to Maintenance and Repair for the blowers and headed it "You gave the lady air!"

On October 9, 1944 with many salutes and last minute shouts of advice on what to tell General MacArthur, the *Marigold* eased away from the wharf and bid Charleston a three whistle final good-bye. The ultimate destination 12,500 miles away at Finschhafen, New Guinea, an island of 312,000 square miles, vast forests and the prized birds of paradise, with their brilliant colored feathers and plumes. When told about them the nurses wondered how the feathers would look in their caps, but they couldn't bring them into the States—legally.

The route to Panama followed the coast to the Straits of Florida, holding wide of the shore to avoid sunken ships. From the Florida Cays and Key West the course skirted the northwest coast of Cuba and to Cape San Antonia and then southeast to Grand Cayman Island. The next leg ran south for 430 miles, passing between Quita Sueno Bank and Cayos Miskitos and then on past Isla San Andres, finishing with a straight course of 210 miles to the Canal.

Hampered by heavy mist and fog, for 350 miles south from Grand Cayman, the Captain took a series of depth recordings to check on the ship's position. The *Marigold's* depth recorder, in the chartroom, showed soundings on a tape of sensitized graph paper and with the great variations in water depth along the route, the sudden changes appeared on the paper and then compared to the area chart gave a good check on location. In some cases the water depth suddenly changed from 400 to only 25 fathoms.

The weather cleared up on nearing the Canal, but had the visibility continued poor, soundings would have indicated the ship's position, as twelve miles out from the Canal breakwater the depth suddenly shoaled from 700 fathoms to the 50 range. Two miles from the entrance, orders were flashed to anchor just inside the Limon Bay breakwater and await an early morning transit.

Six of the medical staff, went ashore to try and arrange for staying overnight at the Washington Hotel and then next day ride the Panama Railroad from Christobal to Balboa to view the big ditch and the surrounding country. Contrary to the forecasters-of-failure, the shore party turned out to be good promoters and the arrangements went through without making any concessions.

The railroad on the east side followed the shore of Gatun Lake, the Canal Reaches, Gaillard Highway, Pedro Miguel Locks and on to Balboa. The travelers were given a fund of information by the Canal employees riding the train and back aboard ship the sightseers gave a good account of the trip to the rest of the staff filling up the lounge. They learned the Canal length to be forty miles, but from deep water to deep water fifty-one miles. The famous Culebra Cut was 8 miles long and 300 feet wide at the bottom with a water depth of 45 feet. All locks were 1,000 feet long, 100 feet wide and the lock wall 81 feet high. They were told Gatun Locks contained over two million yards of concrete. Eight minutes being the average time to fill or empty a lock.

They also were told the saving in miles by using the Canal if the *Marigold* had gone direct from Gibralter to Manila, would have been 6,000 miles, and to San Francisco, 5,000 miles—the reason for building the Canal. After the abandoned construction was taken over from the French by the U.S., the project was placed in the hands of the U.S. Corps of Engineers, Colonel G.W. Goethals in charge. However, Colonel Gorgos, Medical Corps, made it possible healthwise, to carry out the project by draining the swamps with several hundred miles of ditches. He also sprayed the swamps with oil, using 50,000 gallons a month to stop the propagation of yellow fever mosquitos and by sanitation and quinine he eliminated the prevalence of malaria fever; the causes of the heavy death toll of construction workers that plagued the French Company. There is a story that the Colonel's sprayers even put a covering of oil in the holy water fronts at the Panama Cathedral.

The actual construction work took seven years with two hundred forty million (240,000,000) cubic yards of material excavated at a cost of three hundred sixty-six million dollars ($366,000,000). The first vessel, the *Ancon* went through the Canal in August 1914 and ever since, over 5,000 vessels a year have used the Canal, bringing in yearly revenues in excess of twenty-three million dollars ($23,000,000). The Canal toll, based on tonnage, did not apply to the *Marigold* or hospital ships of other nations. All the facts and descriptions on the Canal went into the listeners' diaries as picture taking was not allowed, although postcard pictures could be purchased in Panama City.

The *Marigold* made a seven hour transit and ended up at the Balboa fuel dock to top off tanks for the long haul across the Pacific. Taking advantage of the dock time, most of the personnel headed for the bars and lounges to take on a little refreshment, just to remember Panama City the better. Returning, The Captain was probably the only one to successfully get aboard with whiskey, that is in bottles. It was Black Label and intended for Colonel Barthrup, now a port commander in the South Pacific.

At 2000 hours on October 16th, the *Marigold* left Balboa and started down the entrance channel to Panama Bay. The Canal pilot went off in a water taxi just past Flamenco Island light and the Captain then headed the ship on a course between two sets of lighted buoys three quarters of a mile apart, marking the channel end. With a clear approach to the buoys, the engine room was notified to turn off the steam on deck. When leaving or entering port and in channels, steam was always kept on all deck machinery for emergencies and when clear of harbors or channels the engine room was notified to turn off the steam to winches, windlass and capstans.

The steam was turned off alright but shortly after passing the first set of buoys the wheelman shouted, "I can't stop the swing to starboard and the wheel is hard over." The ship's bow, now pointed for the starboard-hand white light on the outer bouy, the ship still swinging and repidly closing. Grabbing the engineroom telegraph handles, the Captain pulled the port engine indicators to FULL ASTERN—the main engines had not been rung off, so action on the throttle was fast and the ship quickly responded. Fortunately, the rudder was close to amidship when the trouble started. Realizing that they had shut off the steam to the steering engine as well as the deck machinery, the Captain called the engine room and instructed them in no uncertain terms to turn the steam back on the steering engine and on the double. The bow was now swinging left and the buoy only a point on the port bow, so the port engine was put on FULL AHEAD and the starboard on FULL ASTERN, in order for the stern to clear the buoy and protect the starboard propeller from the buoy anchor chain. The buoy scraped along the side with noise like a grinding wheel. The stern, now swinging left, cleared the buoy by ten feet and no banging or hammering was heard so the propellers didn't make contact. The engines continued to steer the ship—one more buoy had to be cleared. When the steering wheel was able to take over the job, the Captain called the Chief Engineer to the office to impress him with the gravity of the loss of steering, whether intentional or accidental. If there had been traffic, a serious collision would have resulted or close to shore, a grounding could have occurred. The Chief left with orders to find out if sabotage was involved—the *Marigold* had an empty and a secure brig.

The Navy guard vessel was informed of the incident although the buoy was apparently undamaged. When clear of the last buoy, the steering was switched to the Sperry gyro automatic pilot (Iron Mike) and the autopilot took over the steering all the way across the Pacific.

The next scheduled stop, now 11,000 miles away, would be through the island-studded South Pacific from 80° west longitude to 147° east longitude. The routing office directed the ship through areas controlled by the Navy, with the first landfall, Malden Island, over 5,500 miles west of Panama. With the help of the south equatorial current boosting the ship along, 400 miles of the distance would be saved by the increase in speed. From Malden the route led past the Phoenix Islands and on to the Ellice Islands, then to Vanua Lava Island in the Banks group and along the Solomon Islands, past New Britian, then direct to Finschhafen in Langemak Bay, New Guinea—twenty-nine steaming days from Panama.

The trip wouldn't be monotonous once the islands were reached, but the first sixteen days with only water and clouds to watch would become tedious to the first trippers. For the ship's crew, with never ending duties, time would not be heavy on their hands, but the hospital complement needed more variety in their present, simple, daily routine.

To provide variation, the evening musical entertainment on the foredeck was started again and movies were shown twice a week on the afterdeck. Projector, screen and films were put aboard in Charleston at Colonel Schowengerdt's request. Films could be exchanged at any of the Army's main ports, so the audience would only have to sit through one rerun. They were old favorites, so there were no yawns. Sitting outside under the clear, bright, starry sky, the pictures appeared framed in a setting of limitless splendor—the largest open-air theatre in the world.

For another event to look forward to, a daily betting pool was established, keeping everyone informed on the ship's daily advance. The closest bet, to a tenth of a mile, based on the noon position report won the money. At 25¢ a bet the pot usually paid twenty dollars and there was a winner every day.

In the routine navigation of the ship, each noon the Captain and the watch officers, sextants in hand, measured the altitude of the sun to obtain the ship's latitude and then the longitude determined from the morning sights was brought up to noon and the ship's position plotted. The twelve-to-four (a.m. and p.m.) watch officer, Roy Robeck, posted the result on the bulletin board—to someone's joy. Of course, the position could not positively be determined to a tenth of a mile, but the figures looked impressive. Celestial navigation using a sextant for sun, moon and stars, was the only way the ship's officers had of fixing position, electronic navigation hadn't come to the *Marigold*.

The navigators announced the ship would cross the equator on the seventh day out and hearing it, the crew asked the Captain for permission to initiate the polywogs. With the great number crossing the equator for the first time and the few shellbacks to defend Neptune's court, considerable trouble could develop. However, the Captain reluctantly granted permission and preparations began for Neptune to board the ship and indoctrinate those seeking permission to enter his kingdom.

Questions were asked by the "greenies" how they would know just when the ship crossed the equator. The Captain gave out the information that the equator was the demarcation line between the cooler north latitude waters and the warmer south latitude waters and when they met at the equator there was great turbulence and this accounted for the story that a broad white band could be seen at the equator. Surprisingly, there was more belief than disbelief—the Captain should know. In order to make his explanation stand up he worked out a demonstrative plan with the engineers, to take place at the time of crossing.

Word was sent out that the ship would cross the line about 0600 hours the next morning, most of the personnel would still be in bed at that time and the effect more realistic. Neptune was not scheduled to come aboard until 1300 hours. The deck officers knew what was to take place and the engineers were to act without orders at the right time. So at 0600 hours, the ship began to shake and vibrate in every part, decks, bulkheads, bunks and people. The trembling lasted for twenty seconds, then all sound and motion returned to normal. The ship had safely crossed the turbulent equatorial line!

In seconds, doors opened and a rush was made for the outside deck, eyes searching astern for the telltale evidence. Froth, foam and suds covered the water, but not in a horizontal line. The engines going full astern were responsible for the still churning water and the heavy vibration—no help was needed from the equator.

The ruse held up for those that wanted to believe until breakfast, then by the time the coffee was served the game was up and the Captain consigned to the pillory. But they all agreed that they could truthfully say they were rudely shaken awake when crossing the equator.

Promptly at 1300 hours, the ship stopped and Neptune—the portly chief engineer—Neptune's wife, Davy Jones and six shellbacks waddled down the deck from the forecastle head, all covered with seaweed and sacking. Trident, sword and instruments of torture were carried by the rulers of the sea. After formal greetings from the Captain and a good word put in for the officers promoting Neptune's language, the court took up positions of honor around the throne. The King read the rules of his realm and the initiation to qualify for membership in his kingdom. The nurses in fatigues were called to account first. The court read off their failings and the corrective measures. There would only be time for ten nurses, acting for all the inductees, to go through the ritual. They were blindfolded, with courageous Mary Stypul first victim, then led one at a time to a chair, strapped down and informed they were to be branded with the trident sign on their forehead. The court had a blow torch going, giving off heat and the smell of hot steel. As Davy Jones pronounced, "I brand you with the sign of Neptune" he quickly put a chunk of ice on Mary's forehead. Her scream was real and piercing. The ice gave the same sensation to the skin as a hot iron. Next on the ritual was an egg shampoo—raw eggs had been mixed up and doctored so they would be more effective. Off came the blindfold, then an act of obeisance to the King and she was given a signed, countersigned and stamped card of membership. All ten polywog nurses were inducted in the same impressive manner and their good nature carried them through.

The court had different rites for the men trespassers. Only twenty-five of the worst offenders were processed as Neptune had other commitments. After blindfolding the lot, they were led one by one to the barber's chair and given a shampoo and massage with sand, then to the dentist chair and pliers put in the mouth and jerked around. The dentist had a pocket full of corn and as he supposedly extracted the teeth, he put in the polywog's hands four corn kernels. They felt quite realistic and there were some concerned expressions. A squirt of ketchup disguised with soy sauce finished the dentistry. As a last cleansing process to rid them of their vices, they were dunked in the canvas trough by the shellbacks.

Just before the end of the ceremony an unlooked-for event took place. Six of the bystanders obtained a case of eggs and from the protection of the booby hatches leading down to the attendants' quarters, started pelting the court. The court took up the challenge and a regular free-for-all ensued, with everyone in sight joining in. Eggs squashed against the house, ports, deck and people. No one was safe. There were no signs of vindictiveness, but there were enough yellow splotches, warning that one thing could lead to another. Since "Cease fire" orders from the upper decks failed to penetrate, the Captain called the engine room for water at the fire hydrants. Hoses were run out by the officers and four streams of high pressure salt water flooded down on the foredeck. The water bath gave some of the medics an idea and they ran out the two hoses from the break of the forecastle and turned the streams on each other and anybody within reach. After ten minutes of water cure, the egg dispensers' ardor cooled and they threw in the towel. A grim Sergeant-Major rounded up the aggressors in the action and herded them below for what no doubt was more than just fatherly advice. The egg fighters paid for the whole case, cleaned up the mess and went on a breakfast-egg fast for ten days. None were hung from the yardarm, but at the next liberty port there would be a significant number stay aboard. For the sake of decorum, the Captain announced that regardless of how many times the equator was crossed, there would be no more inductions. Maybe a night crossing would be the answer.

Warm, fine weather accompanied the ship all the way across to Malden Island and except for an occasional drifting wool-pack cloud to the west, the sky gave no sign of a change and the surface of the sea looked like a sheet of polished silver, with a few ripples for a chased effect. Occasionally rainbow-hued dolphins gracefully arched over the surface, diving back with hardly a splash. In the sailing ship days they were harpooned to provide a change from a constant diet of salt beef and pork and the cautious cook always put a silver coin in a bucket of water with the dolphin chunks and if the coin turned black, the whole catch was considered poisonous and dumped overboard.

After ten languorous days, Malden Island finally showed up broad on the port bow, twelve miles ahead. During the run to Malden the ship's clocks were retarded each midnight a half-hour, for a total of five hours.

Traveling west, if the International Date Line wasn't crossed, would be the way to go to live longer. Possibly that is the reason for Greely's advice, "Go west young man, go west!"

With only the wide tractless ocean on all sides; no buoys, land, or traffic, the Captain had used the leisure time to put together a typhoon-maneuvering board. The idea seemed to be practical since the ship would no doubt be operating in typhoon areas. The board was made of two independent turning plexiglass sheets, the bottom one with a compass rose and the top one with scribed wind-circles and scribed ships in various positions to show safe vessel maneuvering and typhoon behavior. By the time Malden Island appeared, the project was complete and ready for testing, but the Captain hoped he would never have the chance.

As the island slowly came abeam, the Captain switched on the public address system to answer questions asked about Malden. "The island is coral, about five miles by four miles, thirty feet high with salty lagoons inside the many reefs. There is an abandoned settlement and guano works with tramways, used years ago to load guano on small boats for transfer to ships calling for fertilizer. The approach to the settlement is dangerous due to reefs extending 600 yards from the shore. The island, a British possession, is uninhabited and no wonder with little soil, poor water and an average temperature of 90°. It doesn't appear to be an ideal place to start a health spa. We won't be stopping. Funafuti Island, about 1,700 miles away will show up next, the Phoenix Islands will be too far away—that's it for now."

The ship headed a little south of west to pick up Funafuti in the Ellice Islands and the run would be the last long reef-free tangent for many days. Regardless, "Proceed with caution" would still be the rule due to the danger from strong unpredictable currents setting the ship way off course, twenty to fifty miles a day.

In Panama City the Captain had again tried to get good charts of the South Pacific and he didn't have any better luck than in Charleston, but he did get a fund of general information. He was told at the Maritime Administration Office that knowledge on the characteristics of currents in the South Pacific came from sailing ships back in the 1800's and no accurate charts existed for most of the area. There had been no need of surveys due to the lack of commerce. The Dutch had charts for some portions, but they were not reliable with confusing notes on reefs, rocks and islands, many times stating E.D. (existence doubtful) P.D. (position doubtful) P.E. (position estimated)—another way of saying "Approach at your own risk."

During the last three years the Navy had traveled over most of the South Pacific and they now knew all the safe routes, but the information gained remained in the ship's chartroom and in the heads of navigating officers. The Navy was occupied with an exterminating job and not chart publishing. After getting nothing but negative data on charts, the Captain decided to find a likely destroyer in New Guinea that could give him reliable hydrographic information—destroyers knew their way around.

As on the Atlantic side, the Navy routing office in Panama had warned the Captain of detached floating mines and if any were sighted, report their position upon arriving in port. The warning was posted in the chartroom and on the run to Funafuti, the lookout four times reported sighting a mine, but on closer examination they all turned out to be floats, detached from submarine nets. Even so, the floats, round and black, did serve a useful purpose, they kept the watch on the alert.

Fifteen hundred miles after leaving Malden, the ship crossed the imaginary International Date Line. The line in the Samoan Island area ran almost southeast for 800 miles, angling away from true north and south in order to place certain islands in the same time zone. Crossing the line the date on the *Marigold* was set ahead one day to compensate for retarding the clocks in each time zone passed. Otherwise, had twenty-four time zones been crossed all the way around the world from Greenwich, England (prime meridian) the time arriving back in Greenwich would be twenty-four hours off, due to retarding clocks in each fifteen degree-wide time zone. Even if the date line crossing was east and west and not north and south, the Captain's edict remained in force—no celebration.

A day after changing dates, the palm tree tops of Funafuti, at the eastern edge of the atoll, showed on the horizon, appearing like jungle plants floating in the water. Another ten miles exposed the tree trunks and the white-sand beaches. The public address system came to life with the second officer reading off a description of the palm-tree covered island. "Funafuti is 7 miles long but only 50 to 150 yards wide, except for 700 yards at the elbow turn. The atoll was discovered by an American ship in 1819. There is a permanent village of about 500 people. Coral reefs surround the island to the north, south and west except for the passages into the large lagoon. The average rainfall is 180 inches and the winds are light, 10 to 15 knots. The Funafuti natives are reported to be mild and friendly. Except for deluges of rain the island appears to be a better place to be marooned on than Malden. The horizon will be unbroken by land until Vanua Lava Island in the Banks group, 750 miles to the southwest and 14° south of the equator. That's it and keep a good lookout for floating coconuts." The information on the South Pacific islands handily came from a set of books on the history of below-the-equator exploration owned by Wayne O'Day in the accounting office.

On the run down to Vanua Lava the Fiji Islands were not sighted as the course held straight for the Banks group, but the heavy marine traffic was just as interesting. Destroyers passed by at high speed throwing out heavy waves covered with tumbling foam. Drab gray cargo ships lumbered along at 10-knots, some loaded and others with much of the red boot-topping showing, going back to the States for another cargo. The *Portholer* carried a short description of Vanua Lava obtained from the O'Day books. A keen interest in Vanua Lava developed because of the name and the sight of an active volcano belching steam. The island, 15 miles long, 10 miles wide and with a 3,000 foot high crater was easily identified and served as another positive navigation check. Even though the island was volcanic it was inhabited, but with poor anchorages there was very little development.

After rounding the island the ship headed westerly for the Solomons, passing Espiritu Santo, largest of he Hebrides, on the way. This island was listed as being 65 by 31 miles, with mountains 6,000 feet high and a population of about 3,000. The route passed the island too far off to be visible and just as well as the Navy had especially warned of floating mines near the island, a result of the Japanese planting mines fields around the harbors when they were in possession.

A run of 450 miles brought Rennel Island abeam, an island 500 feet high, densely wooded on a raised coral atoll. Rennel Island located on the northern edge of the Coral Sea prompted both chaplains to call for two minutes of silent prayer in honor and in recollection of the lives sacrificed in the battles of the Coral Sea, Guadalcanal, Bougainville and the twenty other battles fought to regain control of the Solomons. A heavy price had been paid for victory in men and ships. The U.S. in the Coral Sea engagement lost the aircraft carrier *Lexington* and the carrier *Yorktown* was badly damaged, but by the victory the Japanese drive below the equator was stopped.

The Solomon Islands covered an area about 600 miles long, 100 miles wide and contained 7 major islands. Guadalcanal and Bougainville islands had mountains 10,000 feet high and some were active volcanoes, but the lowlands were jungle and swamp. They were like another enemy to the Marines. The heat, humidity, malaria and dysentery, added to the formidable terrain, accounted for the Marine's heavy losses. Later on, a *Marigold* patient after reading the *Portholer's* run-down of the Solomon campaigns, told them that crocodiles and jungle rot should be included in the handicaps of jungle fighting in the Solomons—the marine said the only good thing about the fighting was the goal.

To gain possession of just Guadalcanal, the Marines fought from August 1942 to February 1943, when the Japanese were finally defeated. The enemy lost 15,000 men from starvation and disease, resulting from the Navy cutting all supply lines to Guadalcanal. However, the Japanese were able to evacuate 13,000 troops in February, but they lost a total of 25,000 men in the conflict. The U.S. also suffered heavily in ships, losing two carriers, five heavy cruisers, two light cruisers and fifteen destroyers. The Japanese lost two battleships, one carrier, two heavy cruisers, two light cruisers, twelve destroyers. And by losing Guadalcanal they definitely lost control of the South Pacific, their offense now turned to defense.

The Solomon Islands campaign that started in August 1942 actually wasn't completed until the destruction of Rabaul in January 1944, the big Japanese base on the northeast tip of New Britain and the demolition of Kavieng, the base on the northwest end of New Ireland. Four thousand five-inch shells from a destroyer group reduced Rabaul to rubble and six thousand six hundred shells fired in an hour obliterated Kavieng.

The Japanese bases were 250 and 300 miles north of the *Marigold's* track. The course line from Rennel Island headed northeast for 800 miles past the distant islands of Guadalcanal, New Georgia, Bougainville and New Britain—a straight run to Finschhaven, the *Marigold's* destination.

Twenty miles from the New Guinea coast, the Owen Stanley mountains, rising to ten thousand feet, could just be made out. Further to the west, but not visible, the range rose to 16,000 feet.

At 0900 hours on November 14, 1944 the *Marigold* arrived in New Guinea, 29 days out from Panama and burning 15,000 barrels of fuel oil to get there. All the machinery functioned without failure in spite of continuous running. The main engine made almost four million revolutions on the long haul and the first assistant engineer claimed they were ready to carry on idefinitely. But where to, that was the question.

CHAPTER

VII

The patrol vessel off the entrance to Langemak Bay, just south of Finschhaven, flashed an answer to the Captain's inquiry on water depth in the harbor. They advised holding outside Finsch, due to ship congestion and to wait there for orders. The *Marigold's* arrival would be reported.

Everyone aboard was more than anxious to know what the ship would be called on to do along this primitive and inhospitable looking coast, so the arrival of a motor launch alongside with four Army officers brought all hands to the rail. The party climbed the short ladder and stepped aboard through the side port, smiling at the eager reception. One of the officers, a major in the Army Nurse Corps, looked like the genuine golden girl. The expression of awe on the faces of the ship's personnel remained even after the major, with skin and complexion a twenty-four carat gold color, explained that she had been on atabrine, called New Guinea Gold, for two years to prevent contracting malaria. The Colonel thought at first sight she had the most spectacular case of jaundice he had ever seen. Due to the golden side effect from atabrine the Army was again using the old standby, quinine. Some preventive measure she said was necessary with malaria rampant in western New Guinea and some of the islands. She also warned of polluted water and dengue fever. The information was welcome but not very comforting.

The other officers had little to add to the nurse's advice, they were more interested in stateside news. They didn't know just what the *Marigold* would be doing as she was to move on to Hollandia where the Base hospital for the area was located, but they did know the ship would be based at Hollandia in Dutch New Guinea. Before leaving, they talked about their end of what they called the Guinea Hen. The whole of S.E. New Guinea was in Japanese hands when they arrived at Port Moresby and the Nips had to be driven out sector by sector. Finsch Harbor was a U.S. priority target. It was necessary as a base for General Krueger's thrusts at New Britain and at the Jap's most important base in the area, Rabual. Finschhaven was captured by amphibious Marines on October 20, 1943 after a month of fighting and Finsch had been a supply base ever since. The officers were happy to add that in another thirty days most of them would be on their way to the States for a month of catch-up.

Taking along a box of delicacies (mostly food) the shore party pulled away, waving from their launch and the *Marigold* with a good-bye whistle blast headed west. The 500 mile run to Hollandia along the coast proved somewhat different than coastwise travel in the U.S. When passing native villages, set on stilts, outrigger canoes with four bushy heads came out to have a look at the ship and at the many patches of flotsam drifting with the current. The paddlers waved but made no attempt to come close. Not a fibreglass boat, a yacht club, marina, mill or ferry was sighted—8,000 miles from Puget Sound made a difference.

Immediately upon arriving at Humboldt Bay, a motor launch came out with Army and Navy officers and they advised the Captain to anchor inside the bight of the harbor, in order to be clear of the entrance. Tojo had a bad habit of occasionally firing torpedoes at night through the entrance hoping for sitting ducks. Earlier in the year he was successful.

From the anchorage the entire shore area appeared covered with trees and undergrowth, with only a few buildings in evidence and native huts on piling. Not a prepossessing sight, at least it was friendly, but it wasn't always so, according to Major Phillips, aboard as the Base commander's representative.

He told the Captain that General MacArthur, in his campaign to rid New Guinea of Japs had done just that in the southeastern sector, and then continued to work westward to do the same. He invaded Aitape (125 miles east of Hollandia) in April 1944 with two regiments and at the same time, he struck at Hollandia with two divisions. Navy carrier places supported the invasion. In five days the Aitape airstrip and the three Hollandia airfields were taken. At Aitape, 5,000 Japs were killed but only 100 U.S. troops. The Jap survivors fled into the jungle. At Hollandia the Japs lost 9,000 men and only 450 for the U.S. MacArthur had the Japanese 18th Army completely isolated. At Wewak alone, 65,000 troops were hopelessly cornered. MacArthur's strategy was flawless, he put New Guinea in the U.S. bag.

Strange as it may seem the Army could use tanks at Hollandia and on Pancake Hill they mowed down the enemy in bunches. The natives were over-awed by the mechanical monsters, but they also jumped for joy to have the tanks come for protection, the Japs had badly mistreated them.

The natives were a big help to the Air Force in rescuing crews of downed planes. And when the airstrips were in need of resurfacing, hundreds of natives tramped down the soil with their bare feet. The Air Force termed it "The New Guinea stomp."

The Major poured out the Hollandia story non-stop, then apologized for the rapid-fire, explaining everybody ashore knew all the answers and the questions too—an interested listener was hard to come by. With a "See you in Tokyo" the Major asked the way to the transportation and accounting office, he wanted to requisition 600 pounds of beef for the mess of the Supreme Commander of Allied Forces—Douglas MacArthur.

A little later on, Colonel Schowengerdt, smiling like he had a story to tell, brought up the Port Surgeon's orders to the Captain. "We're now a passenger ship." The directive was to go back down the coast to Milne Bay, pick up the 49th Hospital Unit, bag and baggage and bring them to Hollandia. Then what? He didn't know.

During the three day lay-over at Hollandia, three of the staff started a trip to General MacArthur's headquarters at Lake Sentani, six miles inland from Hollandia. For a jeep road the going was good, right through the jungle with the chattering of birds and animals echoing across the road whenever the old jeep had to stop and take in water for a leaky radiator. But they didn't make it all the way to the fifteen mile long lake. They were stopped by an oncoming staff car and politely told to return—there were no visitors' days.

For most of the complement, except for a harbor tour by motor launch, they quickly found out that aboard ship was the most comfortable place to be. The hot muggy weather was enervating and caused an outbreak of heat rash. This time the doctors covered the prickly heat with calamine lotion, the coral color very noticeable on exposed parts. The prickly heat sufferers seemed to get a kick out of being called "Pinkies."

On the launch trip, fifteen ships were counted: destroyers, destroyer-escorts, LST's, LSM's, three cargo ships and an *Alco* Line ship scorched and blackened with a torn and open superstructure from a bomb hit at the Leyte invasion in the Philippines. When later told about the damaged ship and the Leyte bombing, the *Marigold's* complement was surprised that landings in the Philippines had alrady taken place. They assumed the *Marigold* had been scheduled to arrive in New Guinea in time for the next invasion, wherever it was to be. But with no Army hospital ships available, the Navy hospital ships, *Comfort* and *Hope*, handled the invasion casualties. However, in all the Western Pacific campaigns the Navy had provided the hospital ships, *Comfort, Hope, Mercy, Relief, Solace*. It ws logical for them to use their own ships as all amphibious landings were conducted by the Navy and in most of the invasions, the troops were entirely Marines.

The Leyte campaign originally planned for December 1944, was changed to October due to Admiral Halsey's 3rd Fleet flyers in September bombing Japanese bases from Davao Gulf to Manila, destroying 900 enemy planes and 70 ships. With such a crippling blow the Allied High Command felt sure the Japanese defenses were crumbling and the Philippine liberation could be started much sooner than planned.

Judging from the Milne Bay run, both the Captain and the Colonel felt sure that with the Leyte campaign well under way, the *Marigold* for a while, would be moving hospital units from inactive areas to live fronts in the Philippines. It was practical, as the *Marigold* with her immunity from attack would provide the safest way to move the Army's indispensable doctors, nurses and medics to the target areas.

Before leaving for Milne Bay to load the 49th, the Captain went ashore to the routing office, in charge of the Australian Navy, for latest information of enemy marine activities and most important, for charts of the route along the southeast New Guinea coast. And again he was disappointed, all they had to offer were the same old unreliable Dutch charts—probably the same issue of charts given the unfortunate U.S. Army transport *Grant*. Recently the *Grant* tore up her bottom on Suckling Pig Reef in China Passage, not far from the *Marigold's* destination. Coral ledges opened up her plates like a spur on an iceberg.

At the Navy briefing, they warned the Captain to be careful of native canoes coming alongside as there had been cases of small bombs thrown on the decks of freighters. Most of the natives were friendly, but some were still under Japanese domination. The Navy also asked him to keep a lookout along the shore and report, but not stop, for any type of signals coming from the beach or cliffs. Many Army patrols had been lost in the wilds adjacent to the coastal areas. Some had made their way out to the shore and were found in emaciated condition when rescued by Navy craft. In some cases, Japanese had impersonated GI's and attacked the rescuers.

Later, the Captain found a very accommodating navigator on an anchored destroyer, and he brought out all the ship's charts and notes on the New Guinea coast. The charts were old but the lieutenant's notes were recent and indicated dangers, errors and currents. After an hour of soaking up information, the Captain felt he knew what to look for on the run to Milne Bay.

The Captain also called at Army headquarters, hoping there might be crewmen from damaged ships standing-by for reassignment. A number of the Charleston crew, as feared, proved incompetent and some were troublemakers. Unfortunately, no men were available and the Base wouldn't take the violators off the ship. The misfits would have to stay for the time being. Their lack of a sense of responsibility and common sense was a constant deterrant to the rest of the crew trying to do a proper job. The Captain's official logbook had entries of assault, larceny, sodomy, subversion, sadism and refusal of duty. The offenders were logged (loss of pay) and held in the brig if necessary until they agreed to act civilly—for the time being. The Captain's final admonition to them and to anyone not doing his job was, "Remember, this ship is run only for the benefit of the patients."

On November 19th, with the anchor housed and the ship clear of the entrance reef, Hollandia dropped astern and the *Marigold* headed for Milne Bay, 850 miles away. The route was up to the Captain and he elected to pass through the Schouten Islands as a check on position. The last island in the group was easy to remember, it was named Blupblop. At midnight the ship ran into dark brown water, the flood lights above the side red-crosses revealed the discoloration. The Captain stopped the ship as coral at times gave the water a brown cast. Then he remembered from sailing to Alaska, the Fraser River at flood disgorged brown muddy water into Georgia Strait, discoloring the water for miles around. The *Marigold* now being off the Sepik River, the brown color must be mud. A bucket of water hauled up proved it, so full speed again for Isumrud Strait with a bordering island called Bagabag.

From Isumrud the *Marigold's* route followed Viatiz Strait and on past Finschhaven, then across the Gulf of Huon to Mitre Rock, shaped like a bishops mitre. The ship was now nearing rocks and reefs marked "Position estimated" and no navigational aids to help. However, at Cape Nelson, ninety miles further on, two black-can channel buoys showed up, but they appeared to be out of position by half a mile. As a safety measure, one anchor and six fathoms of chain were run out, then at slow speed the ship worked away from the buoys and fortunately, the anchor didn't drag on the bottom—the anchor would have indicated shoaling ahead of the depth recorder in the chartroom.

By watching for changes in the color of the water and for breakers, the picket line of rocks and reefs south of Cape Nelson were safely passed. Soundings south of the Cape were useless, because the steep-to obstructions had several hundred fathoms of water depth between them. Ward Hunt Strait came next and by favoring the Cape Vogel side, the passage was safely run. Then the ship spent the night stalling in Goodenough Bay to await daylight before attempting the reef-strewn channels leading to Milne Bay.

In the morning, and with clear weather, the ship headed for Goschen Strait, passing by islands under cultivation and all fringed with white water. At the entrance to the Strait, the ship turned to line up the steering range markers located on Nuakata Island. The first marker was a cross mounted on a white tripod close to the beach, and the back marker, a painted white cross on a farmer's barn door, set back on a sloping hill. By keeping the range markers in line as the ship proceeded, the side reefs were safely cleared. The small coral island of Hibwa showed up just off the bow and made a good target for the next quarter of a mile, then the course changed ninety degrees for Raven Channel, flanked by coral reefs close aboard. With the sun high and astern, the coral edges could be seen from the bridge wings almost directly below. The color variation, indicating depth was easily discernable. After a half mile of holding to a safe center line, allowing for a 3-knot current, the *Marigold* cleared the last of the coral ledges. The Captain and the watch officers, leaning over the bridge rail, relaxed and lighted the first cigarette since Goschen Strait. The Captain's look-astern clearly said, "Thank God that's over."

Another thirty-two miles and the ship arrived off the Army wharf at Gopi Point. After some maneuvering the tie-up lines were made fast, but only half the ship could be berthed alongside, the stern overhanging a bollard dolphin. Army personnel came aboard in force, eager for a look at new faces and to hear what goes with a hospital ship. Three of the officers knew three of the *Marigold* nurses that had been stationed at Reykjavik, Iceland when they were there in 1943. The nurses, Avis West, Sissy Klingfelter and Patricia Carey, were quickly whisked off to the USO lounge.

Returning in the early evening, they announced that a dance had been arranged for the next night and all the staff was invited—a chance to meet the *Marigold's* Milne Bay passengers. The nurses also brought back the Milne Bay story. They were told that the site was selected as a base for Japanese conquest of Australia and that the Japs had made an amphibious landing at Milne Bay in August 1942. But they met strong resistance from Australian troops and with the help of American planes, were driven off. The fighting then shifted to the Owen Stanley Mountains and the Japs pushed the Aussies over the Stanley's. Then with the help of American troops, the Japs were trapped between Gona and Buna on the coast. The jungle fighting for U.S. troops was rugged and costly due to not having experience in jungle warfare. It took until January 22, 1943 to completely drive out the Japanese and stop and build-up for an invasion of Australia. Ever since, Milne Bay had been quiet and used only as an assist base. The officers expected the camp to close before long or shift to some place in the Philippines. But for now, the *Marigold's* staff was twice welcome to visit at the Base whenever they liked.

Apparently the 49th had little warning about their transfer, they told the Colonel it would be another seven days before they could possibly be ready—now the war would be delayed another week! For something unusual to do, some of the crew thought they would learn how to chew betal nuts by watching the natives. Fuzzy wuzzies, with their black hair, or dyed brown, in bouffant style and teeth stained red from chewing the nuts, walked back and forth on the wharf, apparently confused, not so much by betal juice as by the strange markings on the ship. But after seeing the native's repelling bright red teeth and mouth, the boys decided that sticking to Wrigley's flavors would cause less aversion. Happily, they found a more sensible past-time, less damaging than betal juice—prowling the beaches in search of catseye agates, some were identical to eyes. Roaming the shore was not dangerous—the natives were friendly, they even tagged along like children. Since the native village was only a mile away, they were constantly around the ship and the personnel, smiling and nodding whenever they were noticed.

As the New Guinea campaigns were some of the first to end, the Base had time to fully develop, including a baseball field. A *Marigold* scratch team played a game against the locals, a good field but a lopsided score in favor of the home guards. It was to be expected, baseball practice aboard ship was hit and miss and the *Marigolders'* showed it.

One of the players, a talented enlisted man from the base, made unique kahki caps, with a long stiff bill, flat crown and short sides tapering outward from the head band to the top. The front was high enough to carry a badge. The caps were important looking, light weight and practical for the tropics. The sergeant could have sold any quantity, but only ten came aboard, including one for the Captain, which he said he wouldn't trade for a gold oak-leaf cap.

Great excitement the day before sailing! Word came of a twenty foot python run over by a jeep and writhing alongside a road a half mile away. The dock jeeps were commandered, loaded up and headed down the road. The natives, no doubt thought the gawkers a bit childish, but they didn't know that pythons were seldom seen in the New York jungle. The snake made figure of eight loops, turned and twisted but couldn't make any headway. It was an awesome sight and unnerving thinking of what would happen if caught in those live coils of muscle. The jeep driver that started the show, an MP, put an end to the struggle with his "45". However, the body still squirmed. There was very little road walking after that sight. Traveling by jeep was the only way to go.

The following day, the 49th came aboard to stay. They couldn't change their minds with all their gear stowed in the cargo hatches. In ordinary circumstances, the Captain would have sailed the ship when the unit was aboard, but there was nothing ordinary about dodging poorly charted coral reefs—a daytime passage was a must. Piloting around rocks and reefs, day or night, on the runs to Alaska was commonplace, but they were all marked and of course named after the unlucky Captain or ship that first hit them.

Next morning the *Marigold* pulled out, timing the departure so the sun would be high and show the coral. The Captain went out the same way he came in, so Raven Channel with its coral ledges, visible for twenty feet down, and the run past Naukata Island was made without damaging any of New Guinea's coral. The last reef-bound course followed the Nuakata Island range, but this time the stern of the ship pointed on the range and not the bow. When swinging to the range and looking astern, the upper cross visible on the inbound trip, had disappeared!

With only one range marker showing, running the passage would be risky in trying to clear submerged Revelle Reef. A closer look showed that the barn doors with the white painted cross were open! That put the ship in instant jeopardy. Now what to do and quickly. Steering a compass course wouldn't work with the heavy current. The only way to get through was to estimate the center of the wide-open doorway and keep the ship in line with the lower cross. The Captain's eye was good—the ship cleared Revelle Reef by a hundred feet. That called for hand-shakes all around. Another mile running between small islands and the ship's head turned north for Cape Nelson and the outlying R. and R. patches, in this case rocks and reefs!

Just before making the turn, the engine room was called to turn off the deck steam. Shortly after, as happened leaving Balboa, the steering wheel lost control and the ship continued to swing left and into danger from the reefs around East Cape, the eastern tip of New Guinea. Again, the engines had to take over and hold the ship clear until steam came back on the steering engine. As warnings had no effect and to make sure there wouldn't be a third time, the Captain assigned a deck officer to stand-by in the steering-engine room when the deck steam was turned off. The investigation after the Panama shut-off proved only negligence and this blunder would most likely prove to have the same inane cause.

Crossing Goodenough Bay, a sharp ear was kept when passing the Jabbering Islands, but nothing was heard from the group of eight, maybe the wind wasn't right or it was their silent period. After clearing Cape Nelson, the rest of the northbound run was much simpler and all-night watches for the Captain were unnecessary. On the trip southbound and the other long stretches in tight circumstances, standing up at the bridge rail hours on end was a real back stiffener. To ease the discomfort, Captain Paul Jones, M.D. injected heavy doses of novacaine in the small of the back, it was good for two days. No bill was ever received—one of the advantages traveling on a hospital ship.

All the way up to Finsch Harbor and past Aitape, only small naval craft crossed the ship's course, but ninety miles from Hollandia, a Liberty ship showed up broad on the port bow, apparently enroute from Hollandia to the Marshall Islands. The *Marigold* had the right-of-way and maintained course and speed, yet the freighter attempted to cross the *Marigold's* bow in violation of the rules of the road. The Captain, watching the ship with glasses couldn't see anyone on the bridge or the decks. Something had to be done—the two ships were closing rapidly and on a collision course! Without further delay and to avoid certain accident, the *Marigold's* engine telegraph moved from "STAND-BY" to "FULL ASTERN". Still unable to find any sign of life on the Liberty and collision imminent, the propellers continued to thrash the water to stop the ship. The three whistle blasts should have awakened somebody, but the gray Liberty ploughed on. She crossed the *Marigold's* bow only 400 yards away, apparently with a great feeling of superiority. The Captain followed the ship with the glasses for several minutes, then put the *Marigold* back on course. A ghost ship—not a crewman was seen and the mystery remained unsolved until a month later. The answer came from the Hollandia Port Commander's office. The entire crew, laid out with fish poisoning had collapsed and with the steering secured, the ship carried on until the boilers quit. An LST discovered the drifting ship and a boarding party helped put the crew back on their feet. The ship made port under her own power and with her own crew. Had there had been a collision, fixing responsibility would have been a legal riddle.

CHAPTER

VIII

By December 3rd, the *Marigold* was back at anchor in Hollandia waiting for orders and the Milne Bay passengers were still aboard and enjoying their new lifestyle. Impressed with the friendliness and solicitude of the staff, the 49th's officers were not reluctant to talk about their life in New Guinea. They said the campaigns at Buna Buna, Lea, Salamaua and Madang, were rugged and at times discouraging, largely due to lack of equipment, debilitating conditions in the jungle, and the strangeness of it all. A lifetime of aging in months.

One particular story brought their struggles home full force. In some of the field hospitals, rats were a constant plague and the sleeping personnel were viciously bitten time and again. The pitiful part of the attacks was the chewing, not just biting, of patients' toes and hair when they were under sedation. A continuous watch could not always be maintained. There were enemies besides Japs in the jungle. They said New Guinea was infested by fifty species of rats and they were all voracious.

With another week's wait at anchor, three of the staff had an opportunity to make a helicopter trip into the high interior of New Guinea. Only a day's time was involved so they decided to go. The pilot told the doctors he had the use of the copter when not ferrying the "brass" around the area and, on one of his meandering flights, he spotted a native village high on a grassy plain. Dropping down to eye-viewing level, he saw some interesting sights, so he decided to land the next day with a camera, after working out a plan to impress the natives and to stay alive.

On the second trip the co-pilot went along with a camera and the pilot took extra clips for his "45." An hour's flight and they were hovering over the village. The moves were all planned out. The co-pilot would remain in the plane with the rotor turning and the door open. Upon landing, the pilot, with a box of gifts, approached the stunned natives and scattered cloth, belts, clothes, sugar and rope on the ground; then he retreated until curiosity got the best of the natives. They examined the articles and the women carried the goods to a large hut.

The chances were good that the natives would not turn hostile but, with primitives, any covert move would upset them. The next gesture would be the most tricky. The pilot put four one-gallon jugs on a log and pointed to them with his gun; he fired four times, shattering all four jugs. With the sound of the copter's engine revved up a bit, the explosion noise was not frightening. The natives held their place, spears at their side, but wide-eyed and wary. Then the pilot put up two more jugs and motioned for the natives to break them with their spears. They couldn't; the spears hit but glanced off the smooth, rounded sides, knocking over the jugs. The gesticulating and shouting natives were wildly excited. So far every move and reaction went off as the pilot planned.

Noticing that the natives were confused and probably doubtful of what they had seen, the pilot realized he had to make a big play to establish his reputation. He slipped a different clip in the gun, then laid it on the log and motioned for the fellow with the most amulets to pick it up. After much chattering he did, and the pilot showed him how to pull the trigger with the gun pointed to the ground. Then he pointed the gun, held by the native, directly at himself, backed away and motioned with his finger to pull the trigger. The gun roared but nothing else happened. The native fired three more times and with no effect other than noise. The pilot smiled; the last clip held blanks. The native stood rigid looking from the broken jugs to the pilot. The pilot then bowed and extended his hands and the native did the same and led the way to the largest hut. Picking up the gun and motioning to the lieutenant, they followed along, ate yam paste, took pictures, and returned to the base, sure that now they could return with visitors and be welcome.

After the first trip, the pilot made four more flights to satisfy the curious and prove the pictures were not faked. The pilot's story and the doctor's own descriptions when related to the rest of the staff were classed as a huge joke, but when the pictures were developed the scoffers became believers—not in the native's practices but in the truth of the story.

The pictures when developed showed the men with what looked like various styles of long gourdes, tubes, spouts or the long bent neck on an oil can attached and covering their masculine protuberants. The whole idea of the appendages served the same purpose as the plumes on a peacock, to excite the female. Be that as it may, the pictures were real, the tribe existed, and a lively topic of conversation resulted. Some of the nurses saw the pictures and they said their first thought was the apparent need of surgery and their second and last thought was that the natives could accomplish their purpose better by wearing a skirt. Exposure and familiarity would only breed contempt. The doctors agreed and suggested they make a trip to the tribe and explain the error of their ways!

Orders came at last to proceed on December 10th to Biak, located off the coast of northwestern New Guinea, a run of 300 miles. The Captain went ashore to the Base to find out about what to expect at Biak. Major Phillips told him the Army invaded Biak in May 1944 and met strong resistance by the Japanese. The battle lasted thirty days before the Japs were wiped out. The enemy, ensconced in hillside caves, were impossible to dislodge so they resorted to flame throwers. With no chance of the Japanese returning to Biak, the military units for the most part had moved to the Philippines and the present hospital unit was to follow—on board the *Marigold*.

Ever since arrival in New Guinea, time had lost its importance and, as further evidence, the Army ordered a week of standby at Biak. The Major explained that, with the rainy monsoon season on, the fighting was curtailed and the casualties light so there was no hurry, and the Army decided—and rightly—that Biak was a safer place to wait then Leyte.

The Major showed the Captain a construction chart of Biak and the notes stated there was a barrier reef surrounding the southeastern part with a narrow entrance to a lagoon about 400 yards wide and twice as long. The bottom and beaches were coral. The Army had bulldozed a coral fill into the lagoon suitable only for small boats to load and unload alongside, so the *Marigold* would have to anchor in the lagoon to load her passengers. The Captain didn't like the restrictions of the set-up, but maybe the actual view would be better than the plan view.

A day's run brought the ship to Biak and a Dutch pilot came out to assist in going through the reef and point out the anchorage. After getting both anchors down, and with reasonable scope on the chain, the stern was only 200 feet from the reef. Fortunately, there were no other large ships in the lagoon. Even so, the Captain was dissatisfied with the anchorage, considering the size of the *Marigold*. Then worrying out a week's detention trapped in a dangerous position was not to his liking. He checked on weather conditions right away and, knowing they would deteriorate, decided to shift the ship outside where there would be swinging room and a chance to ride out a blow.

After notifying the Base of his intention to change anchorages and remain outside, the Captain maneuvered out of the lagoon and found a good spot to drop the hook. The Base officers were not pleased by the move, but with the weather worsening and the propellers and rudder only 200 feet from the reef, the Captain felt justified—the safety of the ship and personnel, the criterion. If the ship became disabled under the circumstances, it would be an unconscionable case of mission unaccomplished, and that comment went in the logbook.

The southerly wind continued to increase, reaching thirty knots at 2000 hours. The second anchor was let go with a good spread between. By midnight, the wind force climbed to fifty knots, with spindrift and rain pelting the house, reducing the visibility to zero. The ship plunged in the seas, but not violently, and with her high forecastle head no green water cascaded down on the foredeck. To prevent the ship from yawing—swinging in a wide arc from side to side—and to ease the strain on the chains, the engines were run slow ahead. The blow lasted all night at the same intensity, but the ship held her position. By daylight, wind and sea were abating and at noon conditions were moderate.

After coming through the all-night blow, the Captain felt satisfied he had good holding ground and the ship was able to weather a heavy gale at anchor. Now he could stop worrying on that point. The only apparent effect of the storm showed up on the ports, windows, houses and decks; beads of salt crystals glistened in the sun, encrusted like icing. A good rain would help wash off the salt, but washing by hand would be the chief officer's method.

After the wind contest, with the ship the winner, only a gentle breeze came out of the southwest, slightly cooling as it swept across the hot steel decks, but it was most welcome blowing through wind scoops in the portholes, funneling air into the cabins. Temperature and humidity held at ninety. Outside of personal maintenance, the only activity indulged in was reading, except for a few curious members of the complement who wanted to go spelunking. However, a few hours ashore were sufficient to satisfy their interest in Japanese caves. There was evidence of what took place; the caves had been cleaned out, but not cleaned up; the odors remained.

Daily routine was interrupted on the fifth day at anchor, when an LST coming down from Morotai drew up abreast of the bridge and inquired if a doctor would come aboard and look at four of the crew with a fever of 104°. The Colonel, standing in the bridge wing at the time talking to the Captain, asked the lieutenant if they had any other symptoms. They did—red puffy blotches, muscle pains, severe headaches. The Colonel's face looked more and more concerned as the lieutenant explained. He called over that a doctor would be sent. The Colonel turned to the Captain and said, "Could be scarlet fever, but I hope not."

Two of he ship's staff were handed aboard from the side port. In twenty minutes, they came out of the LST's deckhouse and shouted up to the Colonel, "Dengue!" Relief was evident on the faces of the staff waiting at the rail. Asked about the disease, the Colonel told the Captain that it was prevalent in the South Pacific and caused by the bite of a mosquito and not communicable except by a mosquito. Diagnosing factors were location of the rash, terrific eyeball pain, and mental depression. He said the disease was not fatal, but there wasn't any specific treatment.

After a thank-you by hands clasped above his head, the lieutenant eased his ship away and headed out for Hollandia, wiser and relieved. As the LST pulled away, somebody yelled, "The army's charge for house calls is twenty bucks, don't forget!" It was acknowledged by a blast on the LST's horn.

CHAPTER

IX

On the morning of the 21st, the Biak hospital unit was ferried out to the ship and helped aboard with all their personal gear. The *Marigold* now had 120 passengers for the Philippines, and with Leyte their destination, all the way north the conversation in the lounge centered around the invasion. The Biak unit seemed to know the details, so there was no lack of information to digest.

Apparently two landings were made at Leyte Gulf by several battalions of Rangers on October 20th and the regular Army followed, gaining control of the beaches in two weeks. Then the fighting moved inland to the central mountain area. General Kruger had then brought in 100,000 men on 350 transports, and 400 landing boats moved the troops ashore along the eighteen miles of beach south of Tacloban.

General MacArthur waded ashore from an LCVP right with the troops, and he immediately broadcast a message to the Filipino people, "I have returned. By the grace of Almighty God, our forces stand again on Philippine soil. Rally to me! Rise and strike!"

Admiral Kinkaid's force covered the invasion with six battleships, eighteen escort carriers, eleven cruisers, eighty-six destroyers and twenty-five destroyer-escorts. Japanese army and navy planes attacked the fleet night and day, and suicide planes *(Kamikaze)*—used for the first time—inflicted serious damage. From all appearances, the Japanese intended to defend Leyte Gulf at all costs.

According to a Biak newsletter, Japan's next move was to use their navy to blast the Leyte invasion forces, so they steamed up Surigao Strait, separating Leyte from Dinaget Island, on the night of October 25, 1944, assuming they would be making a surprise attack. The U.S. Navy was waiting and prepared, their reconnaissance planes had spotted the Jap fleet. They were stopped fifty miles from Tacloban. After the battle, the score read: Japanese losses—two battleships, three destroyers and two cruisers. U.S. losses—one destroyer. The Leyte invasion was unaffected.

The possible chance of the Japanese holding the Philippines seemed remote, although the Japanese Army, their submarines and air force could not yet be counted out. Retaking Manila might prove difficult. By early December, there was a report the Japanese, taking advantage of the adverse weather, had increased their Leyte Army by 30,000 men. General Krueger's 6th Army and the 24th Army Corps from Hawaii had their hands full, not only from the Japanese but also from the weather. By November the monsoon rains had set in and the Leyte campaign had bogged down in a quagmire giving the enemy opportunity to strengthen their posiions. With the jungle inundated with rainwater, the whole U.S. offensive slowed down, which accounted for the lack of urgency in getting the *Marigold* to Leyte in November.

By the delay, the *Marigold* was spared the ordeal of weathering the severe typhoon of December 18th, off the Philippine coast. The Navy reported twenty-eight ships damaged and three destroyers foundered with a loss of 790 men. The ships were tossed around by seventy-foot seas. Battleships were rolled like toys, destroyers canted at times to 70°, and the wind force exceeded 115 knots. The *Marigold* in Hollandia felt only the storm's outer fringe because the center originated several hundred miles to the northwest in the western Carolines—the breeding ground of the typhoon.

As the *Marigold* drew close to Leyte, ships of all descriptions crossed the course, going in all directions—destroyers, destroyer-escorts, transports, landing craft and cargo ships. Two Libertys, bound east with boat decks in shambles, gave tragic evidence the Bay was still hot. The *Marigold's* orders called for receiving casualties along the Bay beaches and in another six hours the ship would be there.

Heading into Leyte Gulf the *Marigold* passed over the narrow, but long Philippines Trench, thirty-four thousand feet below the surface. Another fifty miles to Homonhon Island, then a straight run of another fifty miles to one of the beachheads south of the town of Tacloban.

The *Marigold* was advised by blinker from the station ship to proceed, following the buoys, to Yellow Beach for anchoring instructions. The Navy communication ship gave the *Marigold* anchoring coordinates in yards, and the Charleston rangefinder easily located the ship at the assigned position. The location put the ship far enough away from the fleet of anchored vessels to satisfy the Captain, isolation being a prime requisite. Arrival December 25th, Christmas day, went in the logbook, but not as a holiday. The spirit of the day would have to be kept in everyone's mind; the war had to be served.

The beachmaster came aboard and asked the Colonel if he could take casualties right away to relieve congestion in the shore tents. The answer was, "We're ready, send them out; what about our passengers?" The medical corps passengers would debark on the first two LSTs that unloaded patients. The staff would be sorry to see them go; they had become part of the family. Two LSTs came out, the *Marigold's* side port opened, and the ship's litter-bearers went to work. Most of the patients were on litters and covered with blankets for protection from the heavy rain. Some had to sit up due to an arm outstretched in an airplane cast. Most of the ambulatory patients had arm, leg or head bandages covering gunshot wounds. However, there were some cases of hepatitis, jaundice, jungle rot and several mental cases. Loading stopped at midnight, but the LSTs would be back alongside at 0800 hours.

The first night, quiet reigned overhead, and not because the Japs were celebrating Christmas but because the weather was unfavorable. The beachmaster had warned the Captain of nightly air raids and he was right, except for Christmas.

Next day, the number of patients brought out dropped to 100—all litter cases. Three hundred more would give the ship her full load of 765. With the *Marigold* the only hospital ship in the area, the Army requested she wait for a full load. If there were patients waiting, then the ship would wait.

To warn the bridge of an air raid, the radio operators ran a line from the radio shack to a speaker in the wheelhouse and, just at dusk of the second night, the hook-up came to life. A voice came over loud and clear, not excited but deliberate, "Alert red, control yellow"—air raid imminent, fire at will. The warning continued for another minute, then the words were drowned out by the thump, thump of anti-aircraft guns and the higher-pitched clack, clack of lower-calibre machine guns. The anchored ships had little advance warning of the raid as the Jap pilots came in flying low between a gap in the hills and radar couldn't pick them up. During the action, twenty explosions were counted but no fires resulted; apparently the bombs killed only fish. The report next day read, "Last night's attack came out a draw, no ships damaged and no planes splashed." No flack hit the *Marigold's* decks; the bright red tails of the tracer bullets and the AA shells all climbed the sky directly over the main anchorage area.

During the raid on the third night, a bomb made a direct hit on a Liberty in the harbor area. The victim and all other ships had ceased unloading when darkness approached and all ships blacked out except the *Marigold*. The Liberty ship's hatch covers had been left off and a Jap pilot, no doubt by accident, dropped a bomb right into number two hold.

The combustible cargo shot flames 100 feet in the air and burned lively for an hour before being extinguished. Fortunately, no one was in the hold or on deck, but the ship came close to suffering a broken back. The Jap pilot didn't return to report his success.

During the fourth and fifth nights of the *Marigold*'s stay, the ack-acks shot down four planes and three cargo ships were damaged from alongside explosions. The attacking planes, estimated at thirty, were reported coming from land bases—not carriers—and some of them from Manila, 300 miles away.

On the sixth day, December 30th, with a full load of patients and in a heavy rainstorm, the *Marigold* left the combat zone for Hollandia. Two miles from the anchorage a solitary Liberty ship was passed swinging at anchor; the same lone ship was noticed on the way in. The Captain had asked the beachmaster why the isolation and he was told the ship carried a dangerous cargo—5,000 tons of aircraft bombs that nobody wanted because they were not the latest type. The ship had been in the same spot for thirty days and no immediate chance of unloading. With nightly air raids close by, the Liberty's crew could have been nervous wrecks, but they didn't abandon ship. They must have had the patience of Job and the fortitude of Nathan Hale.

The course back to Hollandia, 1,200 miles, was all in the open ocean with no land to sight before New Guinea. The route crossed the usual typhoon path, but with weather broadcasts now coming in from Australia twice a day, the danger of a surprise storm had lessened. The seventy-two-hour forecast was favorable and the comforting prediction was passed on to the wards so the patients wouldn't worry about seasickness along with their other troubles.

The New Year came in with fine, clear weather and the Captain invited the walking patients to come up on the top deck and lounge in the sun and breeze. They came right up and enjoyed peaceful surroundings for the first time in months. The tension, anxiety and nervous alertness so evident on their drawn faces when they came aboard disappeared and conversation now came easily.

One of the group, a Navy lieutenant, asked to see the wheelhouse and the equipment carried on a hospital ship. Talking with the Captain, he said he was on his way to the Navy base at Ulithi via Hollandia for treatment of hepatitis. The Captain asked if by chance he was with the 3rd Fleet in the recent bombing of Formosa and Okinawa that brought on the much publicized retaliatory action by the Japanese. Tokyo Rose's broadcast of the attack bragged of annihilating the U.S. Fleet. The Lieutenant nodded and the Captain said he asked because he understood the air strikes were to divert the Japanese from the invasion of Leyte. The

Lieutenant started to smile and said, "Yes, and it did; our aircraft wrecked 300 Jap planes and smashed airfields and harbors. That was striking too close to home for them, so they sent torpedo planes at us and damaged two cruisers before we got away. If I remember rightly, in her daily propaganda broadcast, Tokyo Rose gloated that all the U.S. Fleet carriers had been sunk that night and instantly." Now it was time for the Captain to smile, then the Lieutenant continued, "Halsey's immediate reply to Admiral Nimitz in Honolulu didn't quite agree with Tokyo Rose and went like this, 'All 3rd Fleet ships reported by Tokyo Rose as sunk have now been salvaged and are retiring in the direction of the enemy'!" That cleared up the situation nicely and officially. The Lieutenant thanked the Captain for the courtesy of the bridge and gave him a Navygram copy of the Admiral's message. Naval officers had a terse but meaningful way of describing an incident and the admiral's message reminded the Captain of Commander Donald Mason's report of an action when in command of a destroyer, "Sighted sub. Sank same."

The four-day trip to Hollandia ended on January 4th and in the usual anchorage. The Army was ready and waiting for the patients with transfer boats alongside as the side ports opened. Twelve hours after discharging began, the patients were all inside the Base hospital, safe from Leyte, but most of them would have a purple heart decoration to remember it by.

CHAPTER

X

O n January 7th, the *Marigold* was scheduled to return to Leyte, but this time without the company of passenger nurses. With stores, fuel and ship supplies yet to be put aboard, there was time for only a mild and belated New Year's party. Beer and buffet was the simple menu for the evening. Fun and games would have to wait for another New Year's, knowing 765 casualties were waiting at Leyte. In the past year, there was much to be thankful for—the war was on its way to Tokyo, and the *Marigold* was doing her part. That was the gist of the Colonel's talk before the last "Auld Lang Syne" of the evening.

Before the events of the New Year overshadowed past achievements, the Captain spent the next day making up a resumè of the ship's activities for the Seattle Port of Embarkation to keep them appraised of the *Marigold's* work. Colonel Leslie Jennings would receive the letter and the Captain asked, if possible, that a copy of the letter be forwarded to the committee chairman of the *Marigold* bond drive so the Women's Clubs could follow the life of the ship they so generously sponsored.

On the return trip to Leyte, the weather for the first time turned abruptly against the *Marigold*. But if the ship had to have a run-in with the weather, now would be the time when no patients were aboard.

The set-to wasn't long in starting. On the morning of the second day the wind rose to forty knots and steadily increased, whipping up twenty-foot seas. Fortunately, the storm was not cyclonic—no chance to use the typhoon maneuvering board—though by late afternoon the seas were over thirty feet high and breaking. Even so, the ship rolled only 20° and with a stable motion, not quick and yet not sluggish. The Tacoma shipyard's ballast was placed just right. But on one of the extreme rolls a freak wave heaved up alongside, reaching two lifeboats high on the boatdeck. A heavy mass of cascading water knocked the boats inboard off the chocks, but they didn't wash overboard—the weight of the water in the boats held them down. The accident was the only one charged against a heretofore kindly sea. After reminding the *Marigold* of its latent power, the sea calmed down and only rain accompanied the ship the rest of the way.

Upon arrival at Leyte, instruction came to anchor close to Tacloban, but also close to the concentration of anchored ships. Not a safe location during a bombing raid. To cooperate, the Captain agreed, but to be safe he planned to move out before the evening explosions started and then return in the morning.

As soon as the ship came up on the anchor, two LSTs with patients aboard eased alongside the open access ports. They made only two trips, since just 300 patients had accumulated. Fighting was slowed down in the foothills by the mud and wet weather—the going so tough transport vehicles bogged down and casualties were carried on litters by the Filipinos all the way to the coast. During the day, five more cargo ships came in, effectively blocking the *Marigold* from shifting anchorages. Though the Captain was given to understand that three of them would leave by 1600 hours, they didn't pull out until the following morning, trapping the ship in an untenable position with patients aboard. A case of "the best-laid plans gang aft a-gley."

With the approach of darkness the *Marigold* was asked to blackout. The Captain refused—immunity would be lost. He passed the word to the staff and the crew warning them of the danger surrounding the ship and that emergency Plan "A" would go into effect at 1600 hours—which meant go to assigned stations and have equipment at hand. Execute Plan "B" only on orders—meaning it's for the damage control party to take action. Follow Plan "C" only should evacuation be ordered. The ship would move out in the a.m.

The rest of the day the tension was apparent in the preoccupied look when questions were asked, but all the staff, medics and crew were alert and steady. After all, the odds were in favor of the *Marigold*. She hadn't let anyone down yet. And they could be thankful it wouldn't be an all-night stand if the Japs ran true to form.

As expected, they came over on time and dropped clusters of bombs, but they also got their wings singed. The bombs were no doubt intended for the cargo ships, but bombs aren't particular when they've been released. The night's drops could be classed as proximity bombs, but on the *Marigold* the stress of waiting minute after minute wasn't in proximity—it was right in the throat. Fragments, shrapnel, rained down all about the ship accompanied by blinding flashes and piercing explosions. The shock waves shook the ship, she strained and groaned in all parts even though the bombs were several hundred feet away. A quick check revealed only chipped paint; the *Marigold* escaped damage and escaped what might have been a calamity. The nearby supply ships didn't take direct hits but they suffered hull damage from the alongside explosions. The AA guns on the destroyers knocked down four of the attackers, but it wouldn't discourage them; they always came back for more.

Unfortunately, to the 300 patients, even near-misses caused great anxiety—a tribulation that had always been meticulously avoided. Next noon, and with no objection, the ship moved to a detached and safer location where the patients, particularly the bed cases, wouldn't be distressed and hospital ship immunity made more certain.

From the new anchorage, some of the ship's personnel were able to go ashore and experience the pleasure and the exercise of wading through a foot of mud in the streets of Tacloban. They found GIs and Filipinos lodged in every building, sheltering them from the deluging rains. The Filipinos they talked with spoke good English, were friendly and grateful the oppressors were on the run. The GIs were curious about the *Marigold*'s comforts—they said they might get a ride on her before the Leyte bash was over! The downpour and the gumbo queered all desire to make more rounds and the muddy medics were back aboard after only two hours ashore.

By January 22nd all wards were filled and the *Marigold* cleared for Hollandia with 300 ambulatory and 465 bed patients. Many of the up-and-about GIs were afflicted with jungle rot and displayed painted hands, feet and head from treatment with gentian violet, their purple blotches showing the same color as purple heart ribbons.

The litter patients' first comment to the medics after settling down in bed was, "What a blessed relief not to hear the constant drumming of rain on the tin roof of the hospital; it was as bad as the Chinese water torture." Most of them wanted the nurses to let them know when the ship was clear of Leyte and actually headed for Hollandia.

Coming up to the Liberty ship with the load of bombs, still in the same position and still intact, the Captain felt they should run close by and give the crew a salute. Drawing abeam he asked on the public-address system for a big turnout on deck and to keep waving until they were well past the anchored ship. The Liberty responded with what looked like all hands waving caps, brooms and flags. No one on the *Marigold* doubted the Captain on the Liberty must have been sorely tempted many times to take the cargo back where he loaded it and mark the manifest, "Refused on arrival"—and it wouldn't be because it was sent out C.O.D.

For the benefit of the patients, the Captain decided to go northabout and close to the Palau Islands so they would be in sight. On the previous run, the ship had passed through the group too far south for the islands to be seen. The Palaus, 500 miles from Leyte, would be a diversion and hold the interest of the patients instead of just staring ahead, looking for Hollandia.

On the safe-passing side of the islands the reefs were close in, so the ship could pass much closer and more of the islands seen than mere outlines. The group included 253 islands but only eight of the largest were inhabited. In passing, the north islands looked like the tops of volcanoes and those to the south much lower and of coral formation. The second island passed, Babelthaup, showed on the chart as twenty-three miles long and four to eight miles wide. Back of the beaches the land appeared to be covered with mangroves but forested higher up. The Captain had heard that water buffalo and pigs were plentiful and could be seen along the shore. However, none was visible; they must have been in the cool forest. But one of the looked-for sights was very much in evidence—sea snakes. Interesting and repulsive, about three feet long, they looked like bright, striped, colored ribbons waving in a breeze, swimming along in close formation. Being poisonous—even if they would have made colorful belts—no buckets were lowered as suggested.

The next to the last island of the group, Pelelieu, was the scene—starting in September, 1944—of one of the toughest island assaults of the Pacific war. Pelelieu was a warren of caves and, holed up in them, groups of Japanese (1,000 in one cave) resisted like maniacs. Again, as in so many cases, flame-throwers were the Marines' best weapon to force the Japanese out into the open. Even with heavy support from naval rifle fire, the Marines were ten weeks in capturing the island.

The northeast monsoon season was on (November through April) for the Palaus, so the wind velocity averaged only ten knots. However, the ship was again close to the breeding area of storms, although the typhoon season would not arrive until March. Another sixty miles and the Palaus were astern, leaving 650 miles yet to go, and they turned out to be comfortable miles for the Leyte "graduates." The GIs thanked everybody they talked with that there was no mud on the *Marigold*'s decks to slosh through and that they had dry clothes to wear and a dry bed to sleep in. What they termed the "Leyte Lament" gave the reason for their appreciating simple comforts: "The rain and the mud. The pain and the blood. The rot and the crud. Makes a GI a dud." Since they always make a fast recovery and come up smelling like a rose, one more line should be added, "But still they'll blossom like a bud."

The *Marigold* arrived with the weather-conscious Leyte patients on January 27th and anchored in the same reserved position. Discharging went rapidly with the large number of walking patients and many of them looked up from the deck of the LST and a made a vee with two fingers and others rubbed their stomachs, appreciating the *Marigold*'s menu after months of K-rations. A young boy, carrying an arm cast, yelled up, "How about going back to the States with you?"—and later on he did! It paid to ask, even in the Army.

With the number of casualties at Leyte on the wane, the sailing date was set ahead to February 6th, a ten-day layover and a chance to have the lifeboats repaired. During the detention the Colonel awarded Philippine Liberation Ribbons to the personnel and later on two battlestars were added. Eventually eight battlestars were awarded for the various campaign ribbons.

Shore trips were not popular with Leyte's rain moving down to Hollandia. However, the base PX was well patronized for good stories and good buys. Another interesting shore diversion for the GIs was eyeing and meditating on the possibilities inside the WAC stockade—the quarters for a detachment of the Women's Army Corps on administrative duty. The WACs helped to keep the mind stimulated.

CHAPTER

XI

February 6th eventually came, and once again the *Marigold* headed for Leyte. Crossing the equator for the sixth time elicited little comment, but the report coming to the ship via the Red Cross about Manila POWs brought on and kept up no end of comment. The sad account revealed that the Japs, faced with losing Manila and with U.S. troops so close, moved 1,600 prisoners from Cobantuan Prison in Manila to the Japanese Islands. But they unfeelingly crammed the weak emaciated men into the closed hold of a small cargo ship. In the floating hell, 300 died from thirst, suffocation, crushing and bashing. Martyrs all. It was not an isolated case; in the first year at Cabantuan over 2,600 of the Bataan prisoners died—the inhumanity of tyrants.

The distressing conversation in the lounge changed on the day before arrival to speculation on the continued presence of the Liberty with the explosive cargo. There was to be a visiting party to go to the ship this time in port, taking along bags of delicacies. The Liberty was rapidly becoming a *cause célèbre*! When the bomb ship did show up, and in the same location, the smiles of relief on the faces of the *Marigold* personnel would have delighted the Liberty's harassed crew.

Closing the beach south of Tacloban, ambulance LSTs met the *Marigold* and came up alongside. The beachmaster, aboard the leading ship, called up to the bridge that his orders were to load the *Marigold* in a hurry because the ship was wanted back in Hollandia. No explanation of the rush was known but the best guess would be that another invasion in another location required a hospital ship. If that were the case, fuel would be a problem. The last time in Hollandia it was not available. But, fortunately, the Navy offered to bunker the ship, so a 50,000-barrel tanker came alongside and pumped 1,400 tons of oil aboard, filling up the tanks. Now, come what may, the ship could steam for forty days.

No air raid occurred the one night spent in Leyte and, with no other delaying interruptions, the embarkation continued night and day. By noon February 11th, the wards were filled and the ship underway for Hollandia. In three trips the *Marigold* had evacuated 2,300 casualties and in thirty hospital operating days those 2,300 patients were admitted, treated, and discharged—a feat for any land hospital.

The officer of the deck on duty at the loading side port reported to the Captain that he had a suspicion some of the walk-ons had rifles with them, done up in packages. He also thought some of the ship's crew had been given rifles from somebody on the LST. A combined search by the staff and deck officers failed to turn up any guns except for one rifle in the possession of a young private with an extensive bandage over one eye. If there were other guns they were well hidden.

The Captain talked to the private, who said he had a particular attachment for the gun. He explained that his company had been on an advance patrol and ran into an enemy ambush. The patrol jumped for protection between trees and high foliage but the Jap snipers hidden in the trees had the advantage and they picked off several men before some of the patrol worked sideways and around in back of the snipers. In the meantime, the patrol took on as many Japs as could be flushed out of the bushes in hand-to-hand combat. American wrestling against Japanese jujitsu (much of the Leyte jungle hand-to-hand combat was learned in the New Guinea campaigns). The firing eased up on both sides for fear of hitting the wrong men. The Japs, when they could get free, dashed off through the jungle but the patrol picked off most of them. The private (first class) stopped his explanation only long enough to light another cigarette. The patrol had the snipers dropping out of the trees like dead birds from the rapid blasts of the thirty-calibre carbines—the clips were good for fifteen shots. The private halted, then went on and said he stepped out from behind his tree trunk during a lull and a sniper on his left let loose with a round that took out a piece of cheekbone and an eye with it. Automatically, he raised his gun. Out poured round after round at the Japs roosting cover. In seconds, not one but two of the enemy hit the ground. Regardless of his wound, he said, his anger at the murderers was uppermost, and to be a good jungle fighter you had to be bitter against what the enemy represented. It was his life or yours. Medics fixed up the wound and the patrol was forced to return and regroup. The private ended his story with, "Now you see why I want the gun that saved my life."

The Captain, with the Colonel's agreement, did see, and he told the private the gun would be kept hidden for now but would be in his possession when he left the ship. The government couldn't complain; an eye for a gun.

Night time photo of the *MARIGOLD* taken during open house Seattle June 1944. In the words of a Seattle Post Intelligencer reporter: "The *MARIGOLD* rides the sea alone, fully lighted at night and the great Red Crosses on her sides and funnel constantly proclaim her merciful mission. They are the only protection she (has) against the enemy on her lonely travels." (Joe Williamson photo)

Passenger nurses earning their AB certificate on the way for duty in the South Pacific. (Photo from collection of Robert Skalley)

Map shows the routes of the *MARIGOLD* during her war time service. The vessel traveled 75,000 miles during 1944 and 1945.

Hospital ships are not immune to all hazzards. 18 people aboard the hospital ship *BENEVOLENCE* perished when the vessel was rammed by the *MARY LUCKENBACH* in the Golden Gate channel off San Francisco. (Joe Williamson photo)

A grave danger existed from guns smuggled aboard with the possibility of the enemy boarding at sea and finding combat weapons. One gun—disguised by being taken apart—could quickly be dropped over the side, but if many were brought aboard and detected, the ship would be liable to seizure so the search continued in spite of the many denials. However, no more guns were found and the trip south was smooth going, with the weather cooperating all the way. The *Marigold* and the weatherman were still on the best of terms.

Hollandia looked the same as the ship came through the bay entrance except for more Navy vessels. The Army group coming aboard said that four of the ships had just come in with Jap prisoners-of-war. Then the shocker: there was a rumor that the *Marigold* was scheduled to transfer the Japs to another POW base. The scheme was absurd and unsafe; it couldn't have any substance. Nevertheless, the Captain lost no time in going ashore to check on the story. And story it was. There had only been talk of quartering the POWs on the *Marigold* for a week, but the unsuitability cancelled the idea. However, the trip ashore did yield positive information for the Captain. The *Marigold* was to follow up MacArthur's latest invasion in his Philippine Liberation Campaign, the January landing in Lingayen Gulf, part of Luzon, Manila's island. The run to Lingayen Gulf would cover almost 2,000 miles and the last 600 through enemy territory. The instructions were to follow usual procedures and for the Captain to use his own judgment for a route. If the ship had a long stay in Lingayen, a secure position wouldn't be a problem with the Gulf twenty by twenty-five miles and good anchoring ground throughout. The *Marigold's* role would not be known until arrival at Lingayen, but with Manila still in enemy hands, and no base hospital close by, it was logical for the Captain and the staff to assume the ship would be acting as a station hospital.

CHAPTER

XII

W ith the discharge of patients completed, loading stores began. Extra supplies were ordered—not knowing where the next source would be—and to make up for combat ships borrowing foodstuffs. Even the Navy tanker at Leyte asked for two quarters of beef. The tanker captain, when he asked for the beef, tried to hold back a grin. "You know the Navy slogan: Not for self but for country!" He got the beef. Next to ammunition, food was the most important item.

The tanker crew must have liked the beef because two days before leaving they arrived in the harbor and asked if the ship would again like the fuel tanks topped off. The answer, of course, affirmative. The tanker remained all night and showed two movies, new to the *Marigold's* crew. Fay Bryan, *Marigold's* Red Cross officer, was a friend of the tanker captain, which no doubt accounted for the movies. Providing for the welfare of the ship's patients and personnel was Fay Bryan's specialty.

As had happened last time, rain precluded trips ashore and everyone was anxious to be underway, so when orders came on February 25th to weigh anchor, spirits revived and the pastime of griping at the rain stopped. Looking back at Hollandia as the *Marigold* left the harbor, everyone on deck hoped New Guinea was disappearing from their lives for good—it hadn't improved with age.

Making the traverse to Leyte was becoming a habit, but instead of heading up for Tacloban at Leyte Gulf as usual, the ship's head swung south down Surigao Strait. If the *Marigold* had been bound for Surigao just a month earlier, the Navy would have held her back for a day until they cleared the strait of the Japanese Navy. To do the sweeping, the U.S. had a clean-up group of six battleships, eight cruisers, twenty destroyers and thirty torpedo boats.

The battle started at 0245 hours and ended at 0730 hours on the 25th. Torpedoes from the destroyers and the PT boats sent the Japanese ships to Davy Jones and without help from the heavy ships. Nevertheless, the Japanese Navy still existed in other areas—including the 2nd Fleet off Samar with four battleships, six cruisers and eleven destroyers. Even so, the Emperor's surface fleet was rapidly becoming a sub-surface fleet.

No signs of the battle could be seen from the bridge as the *Marigold* passed through; the sunken ships were in sixty fathoms of water. Forty-eight miles through the Straits, then into the Mindanao Sea and past the big island of Mindanao to the Sulu Sea. In the western part of the Sulu, two American submarines, just before the Surigao battle, sank three Japanese cruisers, further depleting Japan's navy. Passing Negros Island (shaped like a high boot) at night, the many large bonfires of burning sugar cane on the hills gave a good check of distance off. They were very helpful at night as the prewar navigational aids were not in operation and soundings could not be taken in the great depth of water, 1,000 to 1,500 fathoms.

From Negros, the course led through Cuyo East Pass, opposite Panay Island, and for the next 125 miles the waters were hazardous due to close-aboard reefs and rocks. Without any aids for night guidance, the ship's speed was reduced to make the run in daylight. Mindoro Island came up next and the Captain had been warned to be on guard when going by since the enemy might still be active around the island—even if they had been chased off a month earlier. No shooting was heard, but planes—friendly or enemy—were visible heading north, and what looked like PT boats were milling around close to shore.

Another eighty miles put the ship opposite Manila Bay, but the course held sixty miles off Corregidor Island at the Bay's entrance. Near the *Marigold*'s present position and on January 7, 1945, the last surface engagement of the Pacific war took place. Four American destroyers escorting transports to Lingayen Gulf spotted a Japanese destroyer and gave chase. They scored a hit at 10,000 yards, slowed down and finished her off at 2,000 yards. From then on, the Japanese fought their battles with troops, planes and small craft.

Two hundred miles more and on March 1st, the *Marigold* turned the corner into Lingayen. The picket ship flashed orders to proceed to Dagupan, thirty miles south. As the ship moved down the Gulf, few ships were passed and at the anchorage off Dagupan only a small force of destroyers, transports and landing craft were on station with the landing craft moving supplies to the beaches.

After anchoring a mile away, the port medical officer came aboard and said the *Marigold* would take only fifty patients from Dagupan and eventually end up in Manila for orders. He expected the ship would stay only until March 3rd, then move to some port close to Manila until the Bay would be open for traffic.

The major, when the Captain asked, said the Army's advance down the island of Luzon from Lingayen had been rapid and the casualty list relatively low and that was why the *Marigold* would not be needed as a station hospital in the Gulf. He said the invasion on January 9th was well prepared and surprised the Japanese. With 850 vessels in the attack force and 200,000 6th Army troops for the landings, success was assured, but strong opposition came from the Japanese Air Force. As at Leyte, the enemy used Kamikaze planes to attack the Lingayen invasion fleet— Japan's last and futile method to sink the Navy. The attacks on good-weather days were continuous and inflicted serious damage, principally on the destroyers, although the battleship *California* suffered fire damage and casualties from the *hari kiri* pilots. Some of the suicide planes carried drums of gasoline lashed to the wings and,when the planes hit a wave of fire covered the decks. The *Marigold* received forty of the 200 burn casualties from the attack on the *California*. The Japs tried the same suicide tactics at night with speed boats loaded with bombs and gasoline crashing at full speed into the side of a ship but the guns on the destroyers shot up most of the motorboats before they reached their targets. The fanatics didn't stop trying until they ran out of boats.

During the *Marigold*'s short stay two minor air raids took place at dusk causing a sky-full of noise, but no apparent damage. Many of the bombs hit Japanese wrecked and abandoned equipment strewn along the shore, much to the satisfaction of the gun crews on the anchored ships.

Baguio, sixteen miles straight east of Lingayen, Manila's summer capitol in the cooler mountains, was now occupied by American troops, and all roads including the railroad south for eighty miles to Manila had been regained by the Army. Corregidor was back in American hands and Manila had only a few pockets of enemy troops to clear out. In a matter of days the liberation of the Philippines would be complete.

CHAPTER

XIII

As the major had related, Dagupan did not need the services of a hospital ship, so the *Marigold* was directed to report to the Naval Base at Olongapo in Subic Bay, seventy miles from Manila, for further orders. In raising the anchor from the mud bottom the morning of departure, it was necessary to wash off the links when the windlass wound the chain into the locker, because gobs of muck came up with the chain. At a signal from the chief officer on the forecastel head, the bridge notified the engine room to start the fire pump to raise water pressure at the deck hydrants. After a few minutes he called the bridge on the telephone and reported no hose pressure. Checking with the engine room, the engineer on watch said the fire pump was operating and there was pressure on the line. After another few minutes the chief officer still shook his head.

Something was radically wrong. The Captain sent a junior officer down to the main deck to open a hydrant. Water splashed over the deck, the pump was working. With all the shouting and the delay, an audience had gathered on the wrap-around ends of both promenade decks—nurses, doctors and medics. Words of advice were freely given but not heard up on the bridge with a twenty-knot offshore wind muffling all sound.

Suddenly shrieks did get through to the bridge from the crowd below. Drops and pellets of black goo hit the onlookers on hair, face and shirts. They ducked below the rail but too late, the damage had been done. Gallons of heavy black fuel oil in wind-blown globules splattered the whole superstrucure and onlookers before the bridge could call the engine room to stop the fire pump. Fuel oil could still be seen dribbling out of the deck overflow pipe connected to the forepeak fuel tank. The rain of oil happened because someone at sometime closed the fire line valve to the hydrant and opened the seldom-used saltwater ballasting valve to the tank—both valves opened off the fire line. Water pumped into the tank forced the oil to overflow out of the gooseneck-shaped vent pipe on th forecastel head. A padlock and chain eliminated the possibility of this recurring.

The oil-shower victims' hands and faces cleaned up with mechanic's soap, but four shampoos were necessary before the oil and smell disappeared from their hair. Regrettably, since there was no alternative, the oil-spotted blouses and shirts had to be thrown over the side. The nurses asked the Captain if there was any chance the shower-bath lines might spout oil!

Kerosene, cleaners and brushes failed to remove all the superstructure stains and even repainting was not wholly successful. The cleaning went on for two weeks but for months small pockets of bunker-C oil were discovered. Captain and crew were most unhappy with the defacing their clean white glossy ship received but they decided there was no use crying over spilled oil.

With no further hang-ups, the ship headed for Olongapo—a port new to the *Marigold*, 180 miles to the south on the west coast of Luzon. To arrive in daylight, speed was reduced to eight knots and the lazy run was free of the usual ship noises, an unexpected comfort for the light sleepers.

Rounding Sampaloc Point at 0800 hours, the eight-mile deep Subic Bay opened up. Six miles past the point, the anchor hit bottom close to a sandy beach just above Kalaklan Point, the west end of Olongapo. Damaged destroyers from the Corregidor assault were in port under repair and alike all navy bases most anything could be done for a ship.

The standby at Olongapo lasted nine days and it was just as well. The crew needed the entire time to clean up the Dagupan oil mess. But the medical unit with few patients to look after, had time for beach parties, navy clubs and trading for war trophies. Then to make things interesting for the Captain, the shore police escorted three of the ship's Filipinos back aboard in handcuffs for him to discipline. The MPs said the three messmen were in a service club accompanied by three Navy Filipinos, doing what everyone does in a club. A fight broke out and a general melee followed. The reason for the fracus according to the ship's boys was because they were formerly in the Navy and the Olongapo boys accused them of being traitors by serving the Army. The *Marigold* boys were Moros, tough fighters from Mindanao, so the locals got the worst of the free-for-all, but the army's defenders would always show a few scars for correcting a snide remark. The Captain didn't put them in the ship's brig—not for upholding the Army.

March 13, 1945 ended the Olangapo sojourn and the ship headed for reoccupied Manila—under Japanese domination since the fall of Correg-idor, the island guarding the approach to Manila Bay. Not until March 1, 1945, did the Stars and Stripes again reign over the island. It took all of

February for paratroopers, amphibious troops and a task force of destroyers to recapture the island. During the time the Japanese were on Corregidor they shelled American ships night and day as the passed by, making the run to Manila extra hazardous. But when the *Marigold* passed by on the 14th the guns and the Japanese were silent. There were thousands of Japanese still on the siland—but they were all dead.

In the eleven miles from Corregidor to Manila twenty ships passed by the *Marigold*, many were small navy craft and invariably the *Marigold* received a whistle salute and it was always returned. The special recognition was probably due to the *Marigold* being the first hospital ship to enter Manila Bay, or it could have been due to the nurses decorating the rails.

When three miles from Cavite, instructions from Manila were flashed to anchor in the outer harbor two miles west of the breakwater entrance in forty-eight feet of water. Those were easy instructions to follow and with the ship riding quietly at anchor the last arrival entry in the log book—the water temperature—was taken. The thermometer showed a surprising reading of eighty-two. A decided contrast to Seattle Harbor's fifty degrees.

Manila Bay and harbor looked like a graveyard for ships. Twenty-five vessels were sunk, with bows, sterns, houses and masts jutting above the surface at all angles. The Army Air Force successfully destroyed all the Japanese ships in the Bay area but they could'nt completely sink them in Manila's shallow water. As a result, navigation—especially at night, even for small boats—proved hazardous; the derelicts made a dangerous obstacle course.

To protect life and limb, the bombed-out city had been declared off-limits. The streets were unsafe with intermittent gunfire and falling debris from the crumbling walls of buildings. Pockets of enemy resistance scattered throughout the area, particularly in Intramuros, the walled city, were still fighting the war. Regardless of the skirmishing, the Captain and Colonel were asked to report to the port office somewhere along the waterfront. Ashore, side arms were required for the military and as the *Marigold* was allowed to have a limited number of holster guns aboard, the Colonel accompanied by the Captain, left equipped.

The only small boat tie-up landing they found in use was part of the concrete bulkhead facing Manila's Pasig River and a half-mile upstream. Running on the river with the motorboat turned out to be a gruesome experience. Dodging uniformed Japanese bodies in grotesque forms floating down the river mixed in with patches of broad-leaf jungle foliage caused not a few facial contortions. The Pasig River, dubbed the largest open sewer in the world, looked it in March of 1945.

Fortunately, the temporary port office was found to be in a building more or less intact and close to the boat landing. A trail of footprints showed the route as dust from bombed-out buildings had settled everywhere and given the air an odor like a stone quarry. Looking up the river many buildings could be seen still standing, but many were completely leveled. No civilians were about, only the military, fully armed.

The port medical officer in charge, a friend of the Colonel's, came down in a jeep with an armed guard, to the office for information on the *Marigold's* capabilities. He and the other port officers were impressed with the facts and figures and requested the ship be moved to the inner harbor to load patients for Hollandia, including one hundred POWs recently set free by the army from the Santo Tomas prison camp. After a second cup of tea—that's all they had to offer—and a quick run-down by the medical officers on the location of fellow doctors, the Colonel and Captain left for the *Marigold*.

Absorbed by the impact of all they had just seen, both men remained silent until well out in the open water of the bay, the motorboat zigzagging around the bombed-out ships. "What a helluva waste . . . " The Colonel's forcefulness threw the coxwain's steering off course for a moment. "What a price . . . " His arm swept back over devastated Manila. "Will there never be an end to the same old scourge?" The Colonel's eyes met the Captain's.

"Give the Hitlers and the Tojos an edge and you pay for it—like the Pearl debacle." The Captain thought a moment longer. "You can't hold them back with just talk; it takes a strong arm."

The Colonel and the coxwain also quickly nodded agreement. Then before clearing all the wrecks the Captain diverted their attention to the simple construction of the above-water sections of the Japanese ships they were passing. Not a shaped or fashioned plate could be seen. All were flat, the corners square, no flare, sheer or cambre. Just pointed floating boxes. But that type of construction did enable the Japanese to rapidly replace shipping lost to avenging American submarines.

With the accommodation ladder angling down the ship's side like a stairway, going aboard was quick and easy and reaching the top landing the Colonel and the Captain suddenly stopped, a look of surprise on their faces. Attached to the platform rail was a deeply carved 8x14-inch hardwood board covered with Japanese characters. The deck officer, Fred Mathews, volunteered, "The Japanese took over the ship while you were away and put up a no-admittance sign." The rail crowd all chimed in, "So sorry, so sorry." The Captain remembering from trips to Japan before the war, came back with, "arigato arigato" (thank you, thank you). Junior officer Dick Richings had made a tour of the partially sunken ships and climbed aboard a tanker, saw the builder's plate on a bulkhead, pried it off, and brought the plate back to the *Marigold* as a souvenir. The characters on the board, as interpreted later, gave the ship's name, place of building (Hiroshima), date of launch, and celestial symbol. The Captain mounted the plaque on his desk as a token of the destruction the Japanese brought on themselves.

The next day, March 15th, the Captain shifted the ship closer in and the waiting transfer boats loaded with patients gently eased alongside. They were LCVPs with the usual open deck and high sides, so the ship's gear and lifting box went into action—for the first time since leaving the French Riviera. Loading patients didn't finish until the 17th as the ambulances had slow going through the choked-up city. All the patients from Santo Tomas suffered from deficiency diseases, giving them a cadaverous, wasted appearance. It would take more than the week's run to Hollandia to restore their broken health and well-being, but the necessary therapy would be started on the *Marigold*, both physical and mental. Tender loving care would help to make up for the abuse they were subjected to in three long years.

CHAPTER

XIV

T he trip to Hollandia covering 1,900 miles would be the second
longest non-stop run to date for the *Marigold* in the Philippines and
the Captain intended to follow the northbound route reversed, as it
had proved safe and nothing unexpected had happened. But two months
back there would have been surprises passing Mindoro Island because the
Japs controlled the coast route along Mindoro and they also operated two
airfields on the island.

A Navy Ensign with a shoulder separation, whom the Captain had
invited to the bridge, told him of an incident he had witnessed in December
from an S-class submarine when he was a junior deck officer aboard.
When coming abeam of Mindoro, a high-speed, square-cornered, dark-
green boat shot out from the coast five miles away. The Ensign said he had
followed the boat in the periscope to a point off the starboard bow and two
miles distant. It was easy to track with the sub stopped—not wishing to
disclose its presence. The motorboat covered the water with orange dye
and pulled away to the west and waited. In a matter of minutes, a medium
bomber (Mitsubishi) came into periscope view carrying just underneath
the fuselage what looked like a miniature plane. As the bomber dropped
lower, the underslung plane could be seen to have short wings, stabilizers
and a plastic greenhouse for a pilot—not yet visible. Suddenly the small
plane was released and glided down into the colored water. The plane
didn't hit hard and remained afloat, being no doubt of wood construction.
The speed boat, now astern, took the plane in tow and headed for the
shore. The Captain asked if he ever found out what it was all about and the
Ensign said he did, at the Ulithi base.

What had taken place was a training run for an OKA suicide pilot, riding
a winged rocket that in combat carried over a half ton of high explosive and,
being pilot-controlled, could easily be slammed into surface ships. The

94

device was part of the desperate Japanese *Kamikaze* warfare. The Ensign pointed to a cove on his way out the door, "That's where the Jap boat came from. Those Mindoro OKAs sank the escort-carrier *Omnancy Bay* and three minesweepers. They're deadly. We have a name for their one-way pilots—*Bakas*! It's Japanese for idiot."

From Mindoro on, the trip was plain sailing and Hollandia showed up just where it was supposed to be. After discharging patients, the friendly Navy tanker came alongside and again filled the fuel tanks, showed two more movies and, of course, took aboard more beef.

Manila must have wanted the ship back in a hurry since, less than two days after arrival, orders came to depart as soon as possible. Thanks to the Navy, the bunkers were full. An hour after the orders were received, the ship was underway. Then, a mile from the bay, a destroyer plowing up white water at the bow drew up abeam and flashed orders to proceed to Ulithi. The Captain then asked the destroyer to contact the OIC Army base at Hollandia and verify the change, as the *Marigold*'s orders for Manila came from the office of the Supreme Allied Commander (General MacArthur). The destroyer requested the *Marigold* to stop until confirmation of orders. It was very easy to comply; they had the ship outgunned. Thirty minutes later the destroyer flashed, "Proceed, Manila order priority, good sailing." No explanation of the contrary orders was ever given. Possibly the Navy had forgotten the *Marigold* was an army hospital ship. Ulithi was strictly a Navy base.

The Captain considered altering the usual route and going through San Bernardino Straits between Samar and the southern tip of Luzon and then across the Sibuyan Sea to Manila for a change of scenery, but he changed his thinking after checking on the danger from floating mines. Parts of the northern route were still unswept, so the Sulu Sea route it would be. As late as February the Japanese were sowing mines at night, not in fields but drifters, hoping to catch a ship unaware.

Entering Leyte Gulf a suggestion came up to the Captain to make a side run towards Tacloban and see if the Liberty ship with the unwanted bombs was still in the same place and marking off the days one by one. All the *Marigold* crew had by now involved themselves in the plight of the ostracized Liberty. The Captain was sure the Air Force in Manila could satisfy everyone's concern and curiosity.

The coastal waters off Mindoro had something more to offer than just curiosity. Between Apo Reef and the island, a muffled explosion a mile away threw a geyser of water high into the air, and boiling white foam in waves fanned out from the spot. Second Officer Roy Robeck, on watch at the time, said he saw fragments of some kind dropping into the turbulence. The *Marigold*'s engines were stopped and the entire area scanned with binoculars, but no telltale signs could be seen. From all appearances, a mine adrift with some of its anchor gear still attached and holding it just below the surface exploded when a detonator made contact with some object. Nothing appeared on the surface to indicate a submarine was involved. As the ship pulled away, the Captain looked abeam, "That's one less to worry about!"

Passing Corregidor, the only sign of action was two Navy vessels patrolling the channel—no doubt listening for sonar echoes. Japanese submarines were still running loose and sightings frequently reported. The Navy was looking for the last submarine to sink and the last surface ship to find and destroy—then it would be up to the Army, Marines, and the Air Force to finish off the Japs.

On April 3rd the *Marigold* arrived in Manila Bay and asked by blinker for berthing instructions. A reply shot right back, "Pier 7, inner harbor, at 1500." After idling for two hours, the *Marigold* headed for the breakwater entrance and, with no traffic interference, the Captain had the ship fast alongside Pier 7 with time to spare.

The medical officers from the Port Surgeon Office, on coming aboard, announced a five-day stopover before again loading patients for Hollandia. Five days in port pleased the complement and crew. A month had passed since the last run ashore. The only restriction to roaming the city applied to areas patrolled and posted "off limits," but Rizal Avenue, Quezon Boulevard and Ascarraga were open areas. With no patients to admit until the last two days, time ashore would be unlimited, but only for daylight hours.

Assuming by this time Manila would have crew replacements available, the Captain had Harry Dolley, one of the four quartermasters, run him ashore to call on the Army Port Commander, Colonel John Barthrup, the Water Division Superintendent at the Seattle Port during the *Marigold's* conversion. As the first order of business, the Captain's purchase of Black Label in Panama was set up on the port commander's desk and elicited a burst of "Oh my's." The bottles quickly went into a desk drawer before anybody could come in and stage a holdup. One of the Captain's immediate problems was crew changes, particularly a new chief steward. The medical staff aboard the ship strongly supported a change. The meal quality and service had been deteriorating for sometime and no effort made by the steward to correct the unsavory conditions.

After a review of the *Marigold's* activities and war news, the Colonel explained that the port establishment hadn't yet formed a pool of ship personnel, but he could help by removing the steward provided a replacement could be found in the ship's crew. The Captain readily agreed; he had a man in mind. With the crew question answered, the

Captain brought up problems that had developed with the ship. Three items needed attention. The ship had not been drydocked for over a year and heavy marine growth covered the underbody. The squirrel-cage fan motors in the ventilation system were about worn out and all the engine room auxiliaries needed overhauling. The Colonel said, unless the Navy could find the time to do it, the job would have to be done later on in the States. Nevertheless, he would send out Major Westall, a maintenance and repair officer from Seattle who the captain knew, to make a detailed report for the commanding general. The Colonel's deep interest in the *Marigold* was still evident as the Major came aboard first thing in the morning and spent the entire day on machine inspection. He was thorough, even checking vibration and efficiency before leaving.

Since the second and third stewards preferred to remain in their present positions and not assume the heavier responsibilities, the Captain's choice for a chief steward had been Walter Precht, a personable officer who worked in the ship's transportation and accounting department. He, fortunately, had a natural aptitude for food handling, preparation and supply. He also appeared to be a good diplomat and crew supervisor. The staff liked the choice and the next day the *Marigold* installed a new steward. In just days everyone was smiling again; apparently he knew a well-fed crew was a happy crew. For a chief steward he had an unusual combination of assets, having also a valid undertaker's license!

Conversation at mealtime now switched from food to the cheap way to buy goods ashore. It hadn't taken the complement long to find out that American cigarettes would trade for most anything and, since cigarettes could be purchased in any quantity at the ship's store, bartering became the order of the day. The Manila merchants must have hidden a great deal of merchandise during the Japanese occupation, for suddenly after the liberation the shops—even in their damaged condition—were able to display a great quantity of handmade goods. Linens of all sizes with intricate embroidered designs covered the counters. A carton of cigarettes traded for six fancy monogrammed handkerchiefs; six cartons would buy gemstone bracelets. Slippers, hats, watches, silk shirts, pictures, figurines, art objects, cloth and carvings were readily attainable. The shopkeepers all spoke passable English and they were most attentive. As to be expected, the Americans treated them with courtesy, just the opposite of the Japanese tyranny and abuse. The storekeepers didn't complain of the damage the U.S. Air Force had done to their city; they realized the wholesale bombing of buildings, streets and utilities was necessary to drive out their oppressors. And they were not in any way resentful, knowing what they couldn't do by themselves—liberating their country—was freely accomplished by a sympathetic nation. Many times when wrapping up packages for GIs the Filipinos thanked each one as if he alone were responsible for their freedom.

Regardless of the sudden return of independence, the shopkeepers' food prices were not outrageous . . . ice cream 75¢ steak $3.50, coffee $1.25, whiskey $2.50, and ponycart taxis $1.00 per mile. Public entertainment was nonexistent but there was hospitality in private homes, in some cases of the intimate type, but generally refused due to the unsanitary conditions prevalent in the recent Japanese occupation. Three days of prowling the city proved more than satisfying for all hands, and getting back to routine work and yakking aboard ship again had their attractions.

The main conversational pastime was speculating on the coming mission for the ship now that the Philippine campaign was winding down. The next thrust had to be in the direction of the Japanese homeland, the only way left to go, yet there was no evidence of preparation and sixty days make-ready time would be necessary. Rather than sit and wait, now would be the opportune time to take patients to the States, make repairs, and still be back in time for the next go at Tojo. Wishful thinking, but it could happen if thoughts were things. The carrying of patients part of the wish did happen, but the destination was only Hollandia.

Manila didn't have a full load to put aboard, but regardless, sailing orders were made out for April 8th, so the *Marigold* sailed with 565 patients. While going down the Bay, and much to the gratification of the crew, what ship should be coming abeam but the long-suffering bomb ship from Leyte! Messages flashed back and forth, the Liberty had orders for Manila but not for discharging the cargo, and the crew at last felt like abandoning the ship and going home. The ship's captain said to reserve forty places in the *Marigold*'s mental wards on the return to Manila. The *Marigold* sent a "Roger," then wished them a change of luck, gave three whistle blasts and as the last echo died away, the engines resumed full speed.

Seven times Hollandia had been the ship's destination and no one aboard wanted it to be "Seven come eleven" with the future action sure to be in the opposite direction. Even so, the cause and effect of the devastation just left behind would not be forgotten, nor would the Pasig River carrying its lifeless human cargo.

The run down to Mindoro under sunny skies was pleasant and calm, made to order for the patients able to be on deck. The medics told them of the events that occurred around Mindoro so they were watching for the island to show up. When it did, all was peaceful until opposite Dongon Point; then a small boat came into view dead ahead, bobbing in the water. Coming closer, the boat turned out to be a cabin-forward fishing boat, but not fishing. A small white lug-sail flapped in the breeze, and the easily recognized Philippine flag waved from a pole held by a man on the cabin top. The boat appeared innocent enough, so the Captain stopped the engines and sent for two of the Filipino boys, as his Tagalog (language) could be only gestures. Looking down on the boat fifteen minutes later, ten people were counted including two babies and four children. After much shouting and pointing, the boys had the story. When the Japs pulled out they left very little food and many ruined houses. The two families asked for medicine, rice and canned milk for the babies. They had fish. This was their second day out on the water. Other ships passed but were too fast and too far away.

A case of milk, sack of rice, penicillin, antiseptics, aspirin and cough syrup in three parcels were lowered into the boat. Two of the slim, agile nurses, Kathyrn Adams and Edna Kook, volunteered to climb down to the boat with one of the ship's Filipinos and explain how to use and take care of the medicines. It was considerate but risky, with the boat so unsteady. The Colonel decided against it but he did have the girls carry on through the steward's boys.

The parents' thanks were easily understood. They patted their hearts, then raised their left hands flat out and towards the bridge, and then to the Army men lining the rail. The GIs gave them the victory sign as they pulled away. The red crosses on the *Marigold* now had two meanings, a hospital ship for patients and a hospital ship rendering Red-Cross-type aid. Though not a momentous event, it was meaningful to 1,200 people.

Typical *Marigold* weather accompanying the ship all the way relaxed the patients so they could rest, especially the Santo Tomas POWs not used to just relaxing. Then, after the optimum seven-day run, the ship passed into Hollandia Harbor and dropped anchor where the *Marigold* had squatter's rights. This time, when the medical officers came aboard, they were all smiles; they knew something the complement didn't—but not for long. The *Marigold's* next voyage would be a long one, 6,500 miles to the Los Angeles Port of Embarkation with a full load of patients! The wishful thoughts did become fact—and quickly. The patients soon heard the news and the effect was ecstatic; some of them would have a good chance of riding the *Marigold* home. Should they look worse or better to be selected? Anything to go.

Unrestrained enthusiasm became the order of the day for the ship's company. Just the thought of going home was enough to choke up the most stoic aboard. Every order was carried out on the double and with a smile. Nobody could do anything wrong. Even the conversation was a little high-pitched. Channel fever took hold and yet the San Pedro Channel was twenty-three days away.

Some of the complement hadn't been home for two years, though for most of them it was one year, but the elation was just as intense; even old letters were reread to intrigue the imagination. By this time next month they would be in the midst of familiar faces and places, but now was the time to get the ship on the way. Four days were allocated to discharge, load patients, and take on stores; it could be done if there were no goof-ups.

CHAPTER

XV

Debarking and embarking did go smoothly and the ship was ready to sail after four days, on April 19th. The *Marigold's* favorite tanker was not in port, so a call at Manus in the Admiralty Islands for fuel was arranged by the Navy. On sailing day, the shore staff came aboard to wish *bon voyage*; they were happy for the patients and the ship's personnel, but they would have been much happier if they were bringing their own bags aboard. They doubted if Hollandia would ever have the attractions of Los Angeles.

All the Hollandia patients had been receiving treatment for some time; many were advanced convalescents and would be released from Army hospitals in the States. Others would still have to undergo extensive treatment, more surgery, plastic and corrective, but they would have the comfort of relatives and friends to see them through. Two hundred of the Manila patients whom the *Marigold* had recently discharged came back aboard; they must have had the right symptoms. If the blessing of the *Marigold's* fine weather continued, the trip would be comfortable and exhilarating and they would remember the voyage and the *Marigold* as a pleasant experience, in spite of their injuries. And, to take home a picture of the ship that brought them home, one of the enterprising medics made it easy. For fifty cents, a broadside shot could be theirs. The money went for a worthy cause—the ship's entertainment fund.

The 360-mile run to Manus, a Navy base used as a rendezvous for part of the Leyte invasion fleet, took thirty hours, and a daylight approach was necessary because the island was completely surrounded by outlying reefs, some as far out as twenty miles. The Dutch chart warned, "The Admiralty Islands are only partially surveyed and the reefs and islands off the western end are reported to lie closer to Manus than shown." Some of the charted reefs and small coral islands had the familiar notations of "position doubtful," "existence unexamined," "reported out of position"—dubious information for a navigator.

The *Marigold*'s destination, Seeadler Harbor, had a small island (Hauwei) and reef almost blocking the entrance. But, fortunately, the Navy buoyed the channel and the harbor, eliminating the danger of seven coral patches only ten feet below the surface and inside the hook-shaped reef. After three runs of backing and filling, in order to be heading out on leaving, the *Marigold* eased alongside a tanker (not the fovorite one) and in eight hours of pumping the tanks were filled (not to overflowing) and the chit-chat over between the two ships. With an hour's daylight remaining, the harbor was cleared and the ship out in deep water homeward bound, routed to pass Massau Island and Makin Atoll on the way.

After 150 miles steaming, Massau came abeam. The island appeared to be composed of terraces going up to about 2,000 feet and forested. Many coconut plantations and villages were evident, even at eight miles away. In spite of the current set, the ship passed the island at the distance off as planned. The navigators were always secretly elated whenever the terrestrial observations proved the celestial observations to be exactly correct.

The next traverse, to Makin Atoll, 1,400 miles to the northeast, used up five and a half days of the twenty-three allowed for the entire trip. Fortunately, Massau and Makin were passed in daylight hours so the passengers had a clear view of the islands, a change from watching water and clouds. Makin, sixteen miles long, had several islands inside the barrier reefs. They appeared to be heavily covered with palm and pandanus trees, and no wonder, with a reported rainfall of 150 inches a year. The *Marigold* was given evidence of the fact after passing the largest island, Butaritari.

A line squall blackening the horizon bore down from the northwest, rippling the surface of the sea as it advanced. Opposing ventilators were quickly turned and all weather doors closed. A blinding curtain of water fell on the ship, sounding like a Kansas hailstorm, the water pellets bouncing inches high. In less than two minutes, the decks were running full and the scuppers spouting water straight out in solid streams. The deluge lasted twenty minutes, then passed on, leaving the ship again in bright sunshine. The top bank of lifeboats were half full of water because the canvas covers were off—the usual condition at sea. The small drains on the bottom of the metal hulls could not cope with the flood of water. But in twenty minutes the decks were dry and all the deck chairs occupied.

The next course for 2,000 miles would take the ship abeam of the island of Hawaii, but 100 miles off. For the patients, it would be a week's travel on a limitless, empty ocean with only the imagination to conjure up intriguing sights. For the Captain, the long run would be the first time in several days that he could get a full night's sleep and a full day about the ship. Having his meals in his own quarters when underway, and holding close to the bridge, afforded little time for other than ship's business. On this trip as others, he allowed the patients to lounge about the boatdeck and to visit the bridge in daylight hours, so most of the usually restricted areas were well populated.

After putting a sign on his office door, "gone fishing," the Captain—in shirt and sun-tans and Milne Bay cap—started down the boatdeck looking for familiar faces. In the casual attire, the GI passengers were not reluctant to stop him and ask questions about the ship and the crew.

A career Master-Sergeant, with shrapnel wounds, asked him what captains did when their ships came to port. This was the first time he had ever been asked that question. "Half of the time is spent getting the ship ready for the next trip, and the rest of the time relaxing at home base, enjoying the freedom from ship reponsibility, and doing what comes naturally to a sailor." Then he asked, "And what about your leave time, sergeant?"

After a moment the sergeant looked up at the Captain, trying to retain a grin, "Mine are a little more way-out; when I have a 48 or 72 I do three things and I'll tell you two of them—I get stewed and tatooed." The sergeant rolled up his sleeve, "I'll show you one of them. Look, she used to be a pretty lady and you could see all of her, but when those fragments hit they messed her up and some of my other good pictures too. The skin grafts covered the best parts." The sergeant seemed really concerned. "When I clenched and opened my hand, the lady was at her best. The other arm is worse off. Even my Army emblem got messed up. Look." Quickly baring his chest, the stars and stripes looked battle-scarred, but below the colors the wording was inact, "This we'll defend."

"That's the only one I had tatooed when I was completely sober."

"Well, sergeant, you had it put on in the right place."

"Ya, but this war sure scrambled my gallery." He let out a long sigh.

The Captain touched his arm, "When the war's over, open a tatooing shop and do your own pictures—on others."

The sergeant's face brightened, "Say, you got an idea there; thanks."

Hoping not to run into any more such serious problems, the Captain headed for a group listening to the second steward, Dan Symmes, always good for a dialect story.

When the patients' interest in just visiting and lounging started to lag, and with Los Angeles still over two weeks away, Captain Lanning got the evening entertainment on the foredeck going again. One of the patients, a warrant officer in supply and an Irish tenor, had a clear, beautiful voice.

He was a favorite with everyone aboard, singing "The Rose of Tralee," "The Kerry Dance," "The Lakes of Kilarney," "McNamara's Band," "Irish Eyes," and "Peggy O'Neil." An Irish song always brought the Captain out of the chartroom or his office just as fast as a reef spotted close aboard; maybe it was his heritage—County Roscommon.

Four of the medics formed a barbershop quartet and to prove their title wasn't a misnomer they actually practiced in the ship's barbershop. They were good actors as well as singers. "Sweet Adeline" as always got the most encores. Two of the ship's nurses and two passenger nurses, along with the five-piece orchestra, had a specialty act à la the Andrews Sisters. They went over big but, unfortunately, their repertoire was limited without a music store handy. Also, a boy from Alabama made a good Al Jolson. The fun lasted about an hour and turned out to be the big event of the day, looked forward to as much as meals.

The radiomen had scrounged six loudspeakers in Hollandia and by the time the ship reached Makin Atoll they had run lines from a microphone jackbox on the foredeck to the inside passageways so the entertainment could be piped to the bed patients. The four signal corpsmen were constantly thanked for the sound of music in the wards. Had it been possible to make recordings, the patients could have taken home a souvenir record with voices that anyone would enjoy hearing.

With the evenings well taken care of, the afternoons needed some action besides lounging, thinking and reading, so the daily mileage pool and daily jingle were again started. Any game with betting or prizes involved always had eager players. The war made gamblers out of the GIs, and good ones. The ship's complement had their own type of diversion—planning furloughs. How long a time could they get, what's the quickest transportation, and then—the most thrilling part—thinking about the arrival home, family, friends, dates, cooking, cars, months of events to relate, and the old familiar bed to luxuriate in; minds had few idle moments. There was one big question, how long would the repair work hold the ship in port? The Captain assured the worriers they could count on at least three weeks and maybe more if all the items on the list were completed. They had ample time to visit any place in the forty-eight and not miss the next sailing.

The medics who lived in the east wanted to know if the extra day gained crossing the date line could be held back and used after the ship was docked and they were on furlough! They got the idea because 500 miles west of Makin the ship crossed the International Date Line and the day lost westbound was regained. Another idea not as meritorious as the first one came up to the bridge. For the patients' entertainment, could part of the equator-crossing program be repeated? The idea for the second time was turned down without recourse and they knew "eggsactly" why. As no practical suggestion came up on how to celebrate the occasion, the chief steward served chicken two days in a row to acknowledge the double date.

By early May, the *Marigold* was only 2,000 miles from Los Angeles and the administrative department started their usual struggle with reports and requisitions. The Captain had started on his list of recommendations, but before he got far a diversion showed up in the form of three unsmiling nurses—Alice Grzeskowiak, her sister Florence, and Patricia Carey, the nurse with the heavy reponsibility of the mental wards, were standing in front of the office doorway asking to come in.

Alice, the most determined of the three, started out, "Captain, we understand you don't think nurses are good housekeepers, and we are here to straighten you out. Have you ever lived with any nurses?"

The Captain couldn't help smiling in relief; he thought at least there had been an attempted murder. "No, I haven't had the pleasure, but what brought on the inquisition?"

"Yesterday, Claire Schultz heard you say nurses were too professional and detested housework; they expected meals to be served to them even on private duty and cooking was to be avoided at all costs. Where did you get such silly ideas?"

"I didn't. In the lounge, at the discussion on the farewell dinner someone said, 'If nurses could only put out a meal like that, I'd marry one.' Then I said I had read an article in the *Digest*—please notice I said 'read'—about nurses and other professionals in many cases being unsuited." The Captain held up his hand. "The *article* went on to state what you are objecting to. I didn't say it; I only quoted it."

All three came right out with, "Do you believe it?"

"I'd like to say *yes* just to keep the sparks flying, but in no way would I agree."

The Captain's voice raised in emphasis, "After traveling with you and thirty-four other nurses all these months, I know you would be as good homemakers as you are nurses." The Captain found out—from his reward—that all three girls used different and expensive perfumes.

After having to refuse the invitation to stay for coffee, they left, saying, "It's fun putting the Captain on the spot; you can expect us to do it again."

In his secretarial work, the Captain was down to his lengthy voyage report and thinking how fortunate that, with over 1,100 people aboard, nothing untoward had occurred in twenty-two days. Then, within minutes, word came that a patient—a young infantry captain—was missing, and a morning search of the ship had proved fruitless. The soldier was not a mental patient, but he had suffered from battle fatigue. While the investigation continued, the ship's course was reversed for three hours, and extra lookouts posted, but after such a long interval and so many miles, there was little hope. Not knowing how many hours had elapsed since the accident, defining even an approximate area of search was impossible. Back on course, the logbook entry stated, "missing at sea." For the third time, the same tragic notation, in red, had to be made. But Chaplain Lanning shed a little light on the loss. He said they had talked together several times—just by way of conversation—and that the young infantry captain's mind had seemed over-stimulated and somewhat literary. The Chaplain's impression proved to be true, as he found several pages of penned reflections in a desk drawer. They were thoughts that apparently went through the patient's mind during lulls in combat and not recorded at the time. The Chaplain said they were beautifully written and profound. He wanted the boy's parents to be the first to read them, so they were sealed with his other belongings.

Upon the ship's arrival in Wilmington, the parents were notified and their son's possessions sent to them, along with a report of the circumstances. Then, much to the Captain's discomfort, the parents sent a letter addressed to the Captain of the *Marigold* blaming him in distraught words for not continuing the search until their son had been rescued. The Captain felt bad that the parents would feel any rancor toward him and that something more could have been done. Chaplain Lanning answered the letter and apparently satisfied the parents, as nothing more was heard.

During the final days of the long trip many of the GIs came up to thank the Captain for running a well-found ship and—as they said—all for their benefit. They liked the meals, especially the farewell dinner, and they asked for copies of the menu. The dinner was something special for a ship being away from the States for many months. The steward served queen olives, fruit cup cardinate, chicken noodle soup, grilled steaks—tenderloin, sirloin or rib, depending on the particular mess—bearnaise sauce, peas, corn, O'Brien potatoes, cottage cheese-pineapple salad, ice cream and devil's food cake, crackers and cheese, fresh island fruit, coffee, tea and cigarettes. A going-away present for the GIs.

The Captain got a present too, but it wasn't quite as acceptable. Due to an oversight, freedom from fog was left out of the *Marigold*'s fair-weather contract and so the Captain ran into a real pea-souper 150 miles from the California coast. The course was altered to pass through the Santa Barbara Islands, since the changes in the water depths gave distinctive soundings for position checks—particularly near San Nicolas Island, Osborn Bank and Santa Catalina Island. With the heavy gray blanket closing in, the automatic control for the whistle—set to blast out every two minutes—

was turned on, but reluctantly, as the patients would get little sleep all night long.

The fog hung on hour after hour until coming abeam of San Nicolas Island; then the late morning sun broke through to cheer up the ship's company, most of all the Captain, a little weary after an all-night stand on the bridge. With a thirty-eight-mile run to Catalina Island, twenty-two miles from Los Angeles Harbor, the Captain decided to lie down and take an equal strain on all parts. He left orders to pass Catalina three miles off and call him fifteen miles from Point Firmin, near the harbor breakwater.

Three hours later, the Captain was suddenly awakened by a sixth sense. Fully awake—and in seconds—he was in the wheelhouse. "What the hell!" The ship was headed for the beach at the very end of the island, a half mile away! And the senior watch officer was staring out the window, seemingly unconcerned. But the wheelman, alert and ready for the order, responded instantly to the Captain's "Hard left." The officer turned around, a surprised look on his face, saying, "I was just about to change course." The Captain answered with just two words, "You're relieved." When the ship was safely past the point, the Captain had the chief officer come up to take over so he could go below and dress for the reception at the Wilmington Pier. The case of the negligent mate could wait. Now was the time for relaxing after coming safely through months of hazards and hot spots.

The harbor pilot came aboard outside the breakwater and ushered the ship into the Wilmington Pier. A uniformed band played "America the Beautiful," Allied flags hung from standards along the gangway, and a crowd of happy people on the deck waved and pointed to the patients massed along the rails. The GIs experienced a real thrill—they felt appreciated.

Debarking was not scheduled until 1500 hours and during the wait six Hollywood starlets came aboard to visit the bed patients. Later on three Hollywood stars—Veronica Lake, Ella Raines, and Frances Farmer (a Seattle girl)—walked through the wards leaving autographed pictures. The actresses gave the boys a real lift; they didn't feel left out of the festivities. To liven up the homecoming, Charlie Ruggles and Frank Morgan, standing alongside a dock microphone, kept the audience highly entertained with amusing anecdotes, humorous incidents and repartee. The patter and laughs went on for two hours without stopping. It was amazing—Hollywood's best.

Four press reporters came aboard during the entertainment and they enjoyed the fun as much as the patients, but they did manage to work in their interviews. They told the Captain they had enough material for a series, but they had one final question. Did the Captain have any particular guiding principle in running the ship. Yes, he did. "Be prepared!" That simple motto, learned back in his scouting days, said it all. It was enough for them. The reporters responded as one man with a snappy salute and pocketed their notebooks.

Coming aboard after all the welcoming, the Maintenance and Repair officers, listening to the Captain's "sales talk" for the repairs and smoking the Colonel's cigars, were surprisingly cooperative and agreed to do all necessary repair items for the ship and the hospital as time allowed. The Captain was especially pleased that Maintenance and Repair would make every effort to obtain the navigational equipment he asked for. Before leaving they were able to arrange drydocking for the following week and the ship would remain at the Bethlehem Shipyard for repair of all the heavy items.

The Chief of Port Administration, after making the rounds of the ship, told the Captain that many of the office workers wished to visit the ship and he asked if a guided tour could be arranged for their special benefit. The *Marigold* was the first Army hospital ship to be assigned to the Los Angeles Port so unusual interest developed and the office force wanted to see more than just a name on printed forms. The next afternoon the *Marigold* entertained twenty-five inquisitive, appreciative and enthusiastic young women. Each one left with a picture of the *Marigold* for her desk.

On the second night in port, the Players Club in Hollywood invited the hospital staff to a banquet in their honor. They were entertained by movie stars and film executives. It was a memorable evening and a fitting prelude to their furloughs, starting the following day, May 14th. Luckily, most of the staff had been able to hitch rides on the MATS (Military Air Transport Service). For the nurses, it was easy—the appeal of a damsel in distress.

The next morning after seeing the homeward-bounders off, the Captain headed for the Port personnel office to tackle the problem of competent crew replacments. All the senior engineer officers, two deck officers, four petty officers, and a number of other crewmen were returning to Charleston, some by choice, others by request, particularly the corner-cutting mate.

The chief steward who started out with the ship from Seattle and left in a huff at Charleston was around the Port putting on pressure by talking seniority, trying to regain his former position. Colonel Merchant, Superintendent of the Water Division, asked the Captain if he wanted him back. The response was immediate and negative. The present steward had done an excellent job. The Colonel's reply was exactly right, "The operation of the ship is your responsibility, so the choice is yours."

CHAPTER

XVI

After the ship entered the Bethlehem yard, and with the work progressing favorably, the Captain went up to Seattle to touch home base, report on the *Marigold*, and try the Seattle Port for a chief officer. The Manning Division was happy to oblige. Raymond Fosse, who had left the *Marigold* in Charleston to attend navigation school, would be available and ready to rejoin—which he did when the ship left the Bethlehem yard for the port pier.

The Captain, upon his return to Wilmington the middle of June, started right in checking the repair and request lists, item by item. The new navigation equipment had arrived and installation begun by the maintenance and repair department. The Captain had asked that a depth-indicator be installed in the wheelhouse so he could watch the depth flashing in fathoms and anchor accordingly. The depth-recorder, isolated in the chartroom, made only a record of the soundings.

A dead-reckoning tracer was being set up in the gyro master compass room for automatically keeping track, on a chart, of latitude and longitude by course and speed. A complete weather-indicating and recording system, still in crates, would also be installed in the gyro room for analyzing weather information.

The fourth instrument ordered, a Loran navigation receiver, was mounted in the Captain's office to give digital readings from a pair of long-range broadcasting stations located in the Western Pacific. The readings, in microseconds—when transferred to a Loran chart with numbered lines—gave latitude and longitude.

The four aids were ready for use by the lst of June and the repair and replacement projects were 95% complete. The ship's crew were all accounted for and working aboard under the supervision of the senior deck officers, Ray Fosse, Roy Robeck, Rex Harwood and Robert LaFreniere, the new watch officer. The new chief engineer had reported to the Captain, and talked a good job, but the Captain was uneasy about him and also some of the other engine room crew. He doubted they knew their business but the Port had okayed them.

The *Marigold*'s reputation for taking special care of nurse passengers must have spread to Los Angeles and the Captain was told the ship had been selected to carry 700 nurses across the Pacific! No matter how long the trip, monotony wouldn't be a problem and, as a comforting thought, there was supposed to be safety in numbers. However, there would be a problem keeping everybody busy on such a long trip. "For Satan finds mischief for idle hands to do." And there would be eleven hundred pairs of hands aboard! The hospital complement signed in a week before sailing, looking hale, hearty and ready for work. It was just as well, because thieves had broken into lockers and storerooms and removed quantities of hospital sheets, towels, equipment and stores. With the wartime shortages, replacement turned out to be a long, hard undertaking. The thieves relocked the doors so it was difficult to know when the robbery took place. It must have been someone furnishing a hotel!

To all intent and purpose the ship was ready to sail on July 5th after an over-long fifty-four days in port, but the passengers would not arrive until the afternoon of the 6th. So the extra night ashore would be put to good use. With the rush and activity of the last days before departure, there was little time for relaxing and swapping furlough stories. To make up for the lack, the more convivial members of the hospital staff and their guests spent the evening in Long Beach. Even so, they were all bright-eyed next morning.

At 1500 hours on the 6th, a string of railroad coaches were switched out on the pier and the *Marigold*'s ANC passengers, in fatigues, helmets and full equipment, formed ranks alongside. After coffee from shoreside canteens, they made up two columns and marched to the gangplank, walked up, and 700 of the Army's best boarded the ship through the side port, leaving their shore life for a better life at sea. They were replacements for veteran nurses in the Western Pacific due to return to the States. One hundred fifty nurses would leave the ship in Honolulu and the remaining in Leyte and Manila. The *Marigold*'s passengers' manifest was no doubt the only one of its kind—700 graduate nurses on one ship! A valuable cargo, consigned to the *Marigold* for safe delivery.

One of the first questions bothering the crew after watching so much feminity troop aboard was what would passing ships think with personal laundry hanging all over the ship for drying. However, the problem didn't develop, since no ships were passed close by and drip drys didn't require airing.

At 1800 hours, the *Marigold,* with less fanfare than on arriving, but with more glamour aboard, pulled away from the pier and headed for Honolulu, 2,200 miles away, and again in fine weather even if the passengers were not patients. Little was seen of the nurses the first evening, what with dinner and waiting for berth assignments, but the next day all the lower decks looked like a girl's summer camp with groups pleasantly lounging, reading or writing on all the houses and open decks except the hot steel main deck—a gratifying sight to see them enjoying the complete change of environment, reveling in the freedom from Army camp routine.

On the Captain's daily morning tour of the ship with the inspection party and while walking along the lower promenade deck, they had to step over many outstretched legs and return many smiles. It wasn't too hard a chore in spite of the danger of tripping and falling into outstretched arms. The inspection trip was quickly renamed the "confection trip" and a sudden desire came from all departments to join the group.

The junior watch officers got to know the passengers right away while making their official hourly inspections of all decks, Red Cross markings, and life-saving equipment during the night. Of course, it was necessary in the line of duty to do a little conversing to find out if all was secure. Then their unofficial daytime rounds to check on the passengers' welfare made them even more popular around the decks. The junior officers had orders, not binding ones, to relate to the senior officers during the daytime bridge watchers what all the nurses had told them—some curiosity was involved, but mostly it was to keep abreast of any problem situations.

The boys found out and related that the nurses had asked for overseas duty and all of them had months and in most cases years of nursing prior to enlistment and assignment to Marysville, California, the staging area. None of the girls they talked to were married and their ages appeared to be between twenty-five and thirty. No silver bars were seen on their collars, only gold, and no captains or majors came with them. They were under the supervision of the *Marigold* staff.

Dick Richings, the 12 to 4 a.m. and p.m. junior officer, talked to many of the nurses about their dedication and, in every case, the girls joined up because of a relation or friend lost in the war, or else they volunteered out of patriotism. None of them came for the ride, although they were excited to be at sea—very few came from Coast States. Ship motion didn't bother them, but there had been a few pale faces when the ship first started to curtsy to the gentle westerly swell. No meals were missed and the girls complained of always being ready to eat in spite of never leaving the messroom hungry. The salt air increased their appetite, so they said. Home-sickness wasn't mentioned so apparently it wasn't a problem. After all, they were mature professionals and had gone through separation before.

The junior watch officers also found out there was a bed check at 2200 hours, except for those whose quarters were excessively hot and had been given permission to sleep on deck. In making the hourly rounds, they figured at least half of the wards must be too hot since the lower promenade deck seemed to be fully covered with blankets and sleepers. For the most part, the girls were not well-padded, and how they could sleep on the hardwood deck with only a blanket underneath was a revelation—they must have been practicing yoga. Within the narrow confines of decks, living and utility areas, there was little chance for privacy—unfortunate for the introverts, fortunate for the extroverts. Regardless, if the girls' enthusiasm and camaraderie carried on, they would remember the *Marigold* as a happy interlude between domestic and foreign duty.

While all was joy and light on deck, conditions in the engine room were not. From the first day on, the chief engineer complained that the evaporators could not be made to work. They tried for several days and then gave up. The evaporators had produced 120 tons of fresh water (from salt water) daily all during the past year, so it had to be engineer trouble. The Captain had hoped the former first assistant engineer would stay with the ship, but the pull of home fires was too strong. The evaporators had produced regularly when he was in charge of the engine room. On a long voyage the fresh water situation would have been critical, but with Honolulu only three days away no crisis would arise. However, the chief was informed that he must have the evaporators in hand before the ship could leave Honolulu.

Molokai Island came into view early on the eighth day after Los Angeles and the island was followed to Ilio Point on the western end, then on to Makapuu Point in Oahu and past Koko Head to Diamond Head. The deck rails had been crowded since passing Molokai and now, with only five miles to go, the deck conversation became more animated. With a pilot aboard, there was no delay in being cleared and then, by following the channel range, the ship neaded directly for Pier 8, next to the Aloha Tower. The reception was not as impressive as Wilmington, but there were several girls in Hawaiian dress with baskets of leis among the hundred or so officers and civilians. Two of the medics at the rail strummed on ukeleles and they played well enough to get the mumu-clad girls to do five minutes of graceful rhythmic hula. They were artists and the applause proved it.

As soon as the lift truck set the gangplank at the side port, transportation and medical corps officers filed aboard. Fortunately, a maintenance and repair department officer was in the group and the evaporator situation was explained to him. He promised an immediate cure and offered to give the chief engineer step-by-step instructions on how to make fresh water. Before the day was out an M&R crew had the evaporators opened up, exposing hard packed salt choking the tubes. If the ship's engineers couldn't shock the pipes to drop the salt deposit, the accumulation became hard packed and the evaporators plugged, just the condition the M&R mechanics found.

Late in the afternoon, smiling and laughing at the words of advice about the seduction of Hawaiian music, moonlight and magic, and returning the repeated goodbyes, 150 of the *Marigold's* prize passengers marched down the gangway loaded with gear and boarded six army buses. The girls were still waving from the windows as the buses pulled out of sight; they were a happy lot. The *Marigold* shellbacks told them they would find life in the islands far more pleasant than coping with the rigors of Leyte and Manila. They said maybe so, but they still would prefer to go where the casualties were—a typical ANC attitude.

During the delay in port, shore tours were arranged for the passengers, to pay their respects at Pearl Harbor and view Pali Pass, Waikiki Beach, Hawaiian dancing, plantations, and sample poi. However, only one day ashore for each person was scheduled. But the *Marigold's* own nurses were privileged; they could go and come as they pleased. Being experienced travelers they knew their way around. Two of the nurses, Mildred Barr and Gertrude Bolan, both artistic and expressive, brought back baskets of flowers to give the lounge some color. Antherium, frangipani, bougainvillea, maile, ieie, and hibiscus made the room into a flower garden. The fragrance and the beauty of the blossoms excited the senses and made the lounge the most popular place on the ship. With leis around the portholes, they were suspected of decorating for a wedding. It could have been true with all the comeliness aboard.

On July 17th, with the freshwater tanks filled and with everyone aboard and listening to the haunting strains of "Aloha Oe" rising from a large crowd of well-wishers—men, women and children—the *Marigold* slowly backed away from the pier and started the 4,400-mile run to Leyte. But before arriving in the familiar waters, two checkpoints would be passed, Johnson Island, 700 miles from Honolulu, and Kwajalein Atoll—both listed as way points on the routing.

Even before Johnson Island was reached the evaporators were again making salt and little water. Each day the Captain received reports on all tank and bilge soundings and on the amount of fresh water produced. The results showed the evaporators were adding only ten tons to the tanks and at the present rate of consumption the reserve would be dangerously low by the time Manila was reached. Obtaining water in Leyte might not now be possible due to the absence of support vessels. The evaporators had the enginers baffled, so a program of water conservation would be started to make up for the loss.

The use of fresh water in showers, especially in hot weather, was heavy, so a request was made over the public-address system to use the saltwater line for preliminaries and only rinse with fresh. No economies were possible in the galley but some saving could be effected in wash basins. After a day's trial the daily consumption was significantly reduced. A daily status report was posted and to add interest to the program a gallonage-used betting pool was conducted each day at ten cents a chance. Generally every noon someone pocketed twenty dollars.

On the third day out, Johnson Island, inside Johnson Atoll, was passed at six miles off. The island, an American possession, made a good checkpoint along the way, easily identified by tall towers. No activity could be seen ashore, even the airfield was quiet and the only marine activity was a small cargo ship coming out of the entrance channel. The next checkpoint and the next base would be Kwajalein Atoll, 1,400 miles to the southwest in Marshall Islands and in east longitude.

The days and the *Marigold* moved serenely along with the favorable westerly set of the equatorial current adding ten miles to the ship's daily run. And the halcyon days enhanced by the tropical weather gave the girls a trip to write home about. Lieutenant Doris Schwartz, writing in the *Portholer*, described the run south as an open-air, sun-tan trip, with the night sky a blue dome ablaze with stars, and the ship sailing in a sea of silvery light from the phophorescense flowing from the curling bow waves. Continuing, she wrote—to the aura of fairyland, the girls in groups singing in harmony old favorites added a nostalgic touch to the magic of the evenings—a romance of the senses. Her descriptions were both lyrical and literal, but that's the way it was.

Movies were a twice-a-week affair, but not too well attended; they couldn't compete with nature. The foredeck entertainment of last trip had not been reorganized, probably because it wasn't needed, and then, some of the instrumentalists had left the ship in Los Angeles for assignment ashore, and their replacements were not musically inclined. Having hundreds of girls aboard, there must have been some interesting talent for the Chaplain's musicales, but with people just being interested in people, nothing else seemed to matter. All the ship's personnel enthused over the attentiveness of the passengers; they were open-minded, but not *too*broad-minded. The hospital complement could talk shop with them and the ship's officers could practice a little blarney and know it wouldn't offend.

Don MacKay, the 8 to 12 a.m. and p.m. junior officer standing watch with third officer Rex Harwood, came up with a novel diversion. He worked up a lively interest in the type of hospital cap worn by the nurses after graduation and indicative of the particular hospital where they trained. He had them draw sketches and, of course, one cap led to another. The project went on for days. Caps representing over fifty training schools were in the collection, from the arch-shaped cap with ruffled edge and black velvet ribbon representing Johns Hopkins Hospital in Baltimore, to the flat, low-crowned organdy cap from Saint Lukes in Chicago. Some were like cones with wings at the base, and some fan-shaped—most of them white and, in actual use, starched. Regardless of the original intent, the project drew a surprising amount of attention and complete cooperation. The nurses enjoyed their part and Don had the best of conversation-starters. Wherever he went on deck he was hailed with a fitting name, "Whitecap." The Captain rewarded him for his ingenuity by designating him tour guide for the nurses wishing to visit the navigation area of the ship. He also gave Don the dubious pleasure of explaining to the passengers why a day would be lost when crossing the International Date Line, 600 miles east of Kwajalein.

Seven days after leaving Honolulu, Kwajalein Atoll was expected to be abeam. The estimate was correct but the Atoll was passed at night. Regardless, Kwajalein Island was a Navy checkpoint, so the ship's presence was to be reported. Just before coming abreast of the island, a high-power searchlight sent beams high in the sky, signalling in code. They asked, "What ship?" The answer flashed from the *Marigold's* eighteen-inch blinker, "Army hospital ship *Marigold*, Honolulu to Leyte." Back came the clearance, "Proceed; you look like main street." The atoll, with ninety islands and islets covered with high coconut palms, could have been easily seen in daylight. Kwajalein, the largest island, U-shaped, had a wide lagoon with good anchorage and was large enough for an airfield. Now totally rehabilitated, the island became the main U.S. base in the area after the Marines ousted the Japanese.

The *Portholer* had a few facts in the week's issue on the victory. The campaign to gain possession of the Pacific Islands had been rewarding, starting with the Gilbert Islands, 500 miles south of Kwajalein. They were taken away from the Japanese in November 1943, but not easily. A large fleet of transports, supply ships, auxiliary vessels and 118 warships were involved. Taking Tarawa, one of the Gilberts, was difficult and costly due to the enemy's barbed-wire entanglements, pillboxes, and the Japanese immunity to bombs. Fifteen thousand Marines were used to root out three thousand Japanese.

After taking the Gilberts, Kwajalein came next, a major Japanese base. In January 1944, the assault was underway using six Navy task forces. Admiral Mitscher's group alone included six large carriers, five light carriers, eight battleships, six cruisers and thirty-six destroyers. The invasion force had 84,000 troops available and 300 transport and supply ships. The atoll was literally flattened to copra pulp by naval bombardment. Of the 8,600 Japs who manned the garrison, only 150 survived the onslaught. By February 5th, Kwajalein was in American hands and only 368 Marines were killed of the thousands of troops landed.

The Captain's remark to Rex Harwood, the watch officer, when the signalling was over, would have been a good ending to the *Portholer* article. "You know, passing Kwajalein and reading that it was a place of heavy combat and destruction and now restored and peaceful is difficult to imagine, especially with a mental picture of irreparable damage. Only America could do it so quickly."

Even Leyte was receiving the same type of American rehabilitation. The Captain was told in Honolulu that, in the five months after the *Marigold* had left Leyte, the whole island rapidly became normal and safe. The beaches were no longer known as Yellow Beach and Red Beach, but now identified by their Philippine names, Dulag and Tolosa. Another 2,300 miles on a westerly course and the familiar 4,000-foot peaks of Leyte would show up. A quiet night in the Tacloban anchorage would be a decided contrast to the last three visits. The Captain had been wondering whether the stop at Leyte would entail loading patients for Hollandia. If so, there would be a nurse for every patient! It would be another first for the *Marigold*.

The 150 girls debarking at Leyte made a thoughtful gesture to show, as they expressed it, their appreciation for the consideration and courtesy that made their Pacific crossing so enjoyable. They designed a scroll, headed with "Hail and farewell to our *Marigold* friends. You made a wonderful trip interesting. The twenty-five days will be long remembered." The scroll, bordered with rainbow colors, carried 150 signatures. The ship's carpenter made a fluted frame and the scroll hung in the main deck passageway until someone lifted it two months later.

Forty-eight hours from Leyte the chief engineer brought up another disturbing report to the Captain. He informed him that one of the two fire pumps was out of commission and they could not repair it. The pump went out during a fire and boat drill in the afternoon. The evaporators and now the fire pump!

On August 3rd the anchor hit the mud off Dulag and an LSM came alongside with medical corps officers. They asked the nurses to stay aboard overnight because their camp quarters would not be ready until morning. There wasn't any objection to this since the *au revoir* embraces could now be done a second time. The replay, with song and dance, lasted until the next day, but by 1100 hours on the 4th, the Leyte contingent was on their way to Tocloban and the *Marigold*, with closed side port and raised anchor, was on the way to Manila. Another 660 miles had to pass by the keel and then the passenger ship *Marigold* could again become the hospital ship *Marigold*. Leyte had no patients to send out; they no longer transferred patients to Hollandia. The local hospital was self-sufficient.

The nurses ticketed for Manila, not to be outdone by the Leyte group, asked to be put on ship's work, so Chief Officer Ray Fosse gave them buckets of soogee (washing powder and water), buckets of clean water, and soft rags. The inside of the bulwarks, the house bulkheads and pipe railings never received such thorough and careful washing. No slopping, no holidays left and no griping even when the skin on their fingers shriveled from the strong washing powder. Mr. Fosse told the ten girls elected to do the work that he would give them a seaman's discharge certificate at Manila, with ability marked V.G., character V.G., seaman-ship V.G., and signed by the Captain—they would be able to go to sea if the nursing profession became overcrowded.

On the second day out of Leyte, the engine room hoodoo struck again. It was during the daily early-morning deck washdown. The two hydrant hoses went limp—no pressure! the boatswain called the mate and he called the engine room—the second fire pump joined the first on the disabled list. Fortunately, a crossover on a bilge pump provided substitute fire protection, easing a dangerous situation. The Captain hated to think of what would happen if the sanitary pump went the way of the fire pumps! With bad luck persisting in the engine room, the Captain glanced at the main engine revolution counters each time he came in the wheelhouse to see if the revolutions per minute were holding at ninety. The main engines could be the next to break down and that would be disastrous. The Captain must have had some distressing premonition, as he was on edge the rest of the way to Manila.

CHAPTER

17

However, nothing untoward happened to upset the even tenor of the last 400 miles; even passing Mindoro the sea was asleep and all naval activity had ceased around Corregidor. There were no challenges until three miles from Manila Bay, and then only to receive anchoring instructions, debarking time and method. According to orders the passengers were to remain aboard for five more days, so the Captain asked permission to go alongside the station tanker for 250,000 gallons of fresh water. The tanks were down to half their capacity and a water problem would exist until the evaporators started producing. Permission was granted to tie up on the starboard side of the tanker; a transport occupied the port side.

The *Marigold* had been stopped during the back and forth messages on the blinker and the Captain now ordered slow ahead on both engines. Only the starboard engine responded. Now what was wrong? The engine room called and informed that the throttle on the port engine was inoperative and could not be immediately repaired! Unknown to the Captain, the throttle had been causing trouble at Leyte. The watch officer hung up the phone in time to hear some very salty expletives from the Captain, and no wonder, with a strong wind setting the ship against the tanker and the starboard engine, when backing, further setting the ship over. The anchor could not be used to dredge against due to the debris on the harbor bottom, so the Captain turned the ship to come in from the opposite angle. Thirty minutes of maneuvering had the *Marigold* alongside and the hoses connected. Then, four hours later, with 1,000 tons of the Navy's evaporated water aboard, the ship was at anchor in the same spot as last voyage. After cooling down some, the Captain decided to forego having words with the chief engineer as his time aboard the *Marigold* was down to hours.

First thing the next morning the Captain went ashore and called on the

Army Port Commander, again Colonel John Barthrop. After hearing of the conditions in the engine room and what might happen to impair the operation of the ship, the Colonel didn't hesitate to provide a chief and assistant. The men he had in mind were from a torpedoed Dutch ship. They had good reputations and records, so the Captain met with them and he told the Colonel later that their English left a lot to be desired, but not their knowledge of ships' machinery. They replaced the chief and first assistant the next day and in one week the evaporators, pumps and throttle all were in working order. Glory hallelujah! The Captain's relief was apparent in the return of his good humor. Deteriorating conditions in the engine room had been a constant source of worry as he assumed the *Marigold* would be going on the final big push on the Japanese homeland and he wanted the ship to be ready to go in all respects. The Captain learned later that the Los Angeles chief engineer had not been to sea for ten years and was recently working as a stationary engineer in an office building!

The ship was scheduled to leave Manila on August 20th, but the destination was not divulged. There would be a wait of two weeks. Even so, the time would have gone quickly had the passengers remained aboard but, the day after anchoring, the nurses were transferred to shore by barge and on to temporary quarters in a rural monastery to await assignment. There was little of the usual leave-taking when the girls departed because many of the ship's personnel intended to call on them to see if they had exchanged uniforms for habits. The ten fledgling female sailors made sure they had their discharges in their shoulder bags, along with other important papers, when they went ashore.

During the next thirteen days in port, since there was little to see except ruins, the shore parties spent most of their time trading and bartering. Little money changed hands, since cigarettes and PX items were still the means of exchange for beautiful handworked linens and shirts. Surprisingly, many fine jewelry pieces were brought out of hiding and traded. Sugar, flour and canned milk could buy any high-value article, but government foodstuffs were not to be had for purchase and barter. Even so, everyone aboard had many pieces of Philippine craft and art to take home, and every piece had a story to tell.

Japanese occupation money was available by the bundle for cigarettes by the package. The money was dirty and not desirable, even for souvenirs, so few samples came aboard. However, four of the medical attendants did take along a number of two-inch-thick bundles—whether by accident or design, they made good use of them later on.

The high point of the time at anchor came on August 15th. The day hostilities ended. A day celebrated like the 4th of July. Ashore, fireworks unearthed for the occasion were set off. Explosions, whistles and revelry lasted all night. On the *Marigold,* to celebrate the end of the war in Europe and the just-received word that Emperor Hirohito had issued a cease-fire order, blue parachute flares were shot off and floated in the sky. Yellow and green smoke floats held on a line covered the water around the ship. An extra beer ration went the rounds. With every passing ship and boat, cheers and hurrahs were shouted back and forth. The momentous event, long awaited through many trying months, finally happened—the war was over!

To once again be able to think, work, play and live normally without the fear of tragedy striking was almost beyond belief. But it was easy to believe that a complete reversal of attitude would be necessary—from "kill or be killed" to "live and let live." With the changes in thinking, ship conversation for the next days dwelt on the joys of peace, of no more furloughs—only discharges—and then to be your own man. But it didn't take long to recognize, after listening to Tokyo Rose's broadcast, that a cease-fire didn't mean quitting. It was true in the *Marigold's* case; there were patients still waiting in the hospitals for them to take back to the States.

On August 18th, a surprise was handed the ship; she was still to be a passenger vessel. The 42nd General Hospital personnel, with bag, baggage and equipment, would come aboard the next day for transportation to Okinawa. With the recently conquered island as a destination, only 850 miles from Tokyo, the *Marigold* would be getting closer to the finale. The last act of the five-part tragedy—Pearl Harbor, the Pacific Islands, Philippines, Iwo Jima-Okinaa, and the climax: Japan.

Three unscheduled passengers came aboard sometime before midnight ahead of the scheduled passengers, and they were destined to spend the balance of the night in the ship's poorest accommodation—the brig. Along about 2300 hoiurs, the smoke detector alarm sounded off in the wheelhouse, summoning everyone in the Captain's and officers' quarters, just aft of the bridge, to the indicator box. The tab was down for the tween-deck storeroom below number four hatch. Smoke meant fire and fire meant danger. The chief and four other deck officers headed on the double for the booby hatch, leading to the tween-decks. In five minutes they were out on deck, not apparing too excited and forcibly escorting three Filipino women. Entering the wheelhouse, two comely young girls and a very old woman started talking louder and faster. Holding up both hands, the Captain stopped them and sent for his Filipino steward. In the meantime, the officers said they had found the old lady puffing on a rank cheroot right below the sensor and in time the smoke apparently was thick enough to activate the alarm!

Twenty mintues after the question-and-answer period, José, the steward, with a feigned serious look on his face, explained the presence of the would-be stowaways. They wanted to leave Manila on a passenger ship and the *Marigold* looked good; they also knew there were many men living up forward. José was positive they intended to go into business. The old lady claimed the girls were her daughters; it was obvious they were not. The old lady had hired a boat to scull them to the ship and, fortunately for the women, the Jacobs Ladder and staging used by the crew in painting the hull were still over the side, the work unfinished.

The Captain was so relieved the B-girls were discovered before the ship put to sea—the ship being responsible for stowaways— that he had José bring them a lunch and blankets. The brig was under the forecastle-head, completely isolated, and a plan was made to set them ashore at daybreak, so the razzing couldn't start until the feat was accomplished. That afternoon, very close attention was given to each of the passengers from the 42nd as they came aboard. The only evidence, verbal or visual, of the *fille de joie* incident being known was a red light painted on the booby hatch.

CHAPTER

XVIII

From Manila the course followed up the Luzon coast past Lingayen Gulf and Cape Bojeador at the north end, then through Luzon Strait to Bashi Channel and northeast to Okinawa, passing Formosa on the way. The island provided bases for Japanese suicide planes that caused so much havoc at Iwo and Okinawa. The Iwo attack took place in February-March and Okinawa through April, May and June. During the fury of the Okinawa invasion, a kamikaze flew into the after-superstructure of the Navy hospital ship *Comfort*, killing two and inflicting extensive ship damage. Whether intentional or accidental would never be known. The *Marigold* was headed for Naha, near Buckner Bay, named in honor of General Simon Buckner, the commander of the Okinawa invasion troops. Regrettably, the General had been killed by a shellburst just three days before the island surrendered.

The hills of southern Okinawa were not a prominent feature, being only 400 to 500 feet high, but Okinawa was easily identified by the many small islands (Kerama Retto) off the west coast. Reefs could be seen all along the shoreline for the sixteen miles to Buckner Bay. Orders from the picket boat were to anchor in the transport area in a twenty-three fathom spot. Wrecked ships, from destroyers to LSTs, could be seen strewn along the beach and in shallow water. The concentration of Japanese artillery had been entrenched in the southern part of the sixty-mile-long island, and the foreshore was within easy range of their guns.

Medical officers came aboard to arrange debarking the 42nd at Naha, the small port six miles south of Buckner Bay. The *Marigold* was to shift in the morning to a point just off Naha, unload and leave on the 26th for the Tokyo-Yokohama area.

The port surgeon's representative, Major Porter, informed the Captain that blackout regulations were still being observed, even if the air raids had

122

ceased. Asked about the Japanese resistance at Iwo and Okinawa, the Major shook his head and said, "Rugged." He went on and gave the Captain a rundown. The Major was in on both landings. With coffee in one hand and a cigarette in the other, he explained that—even if Iwo was only five miles long—taking it was a difficult feat because the island was composed of lava and granite, impervious to bombing. The Japs were in caves and dugouts and had to be rooted out place by place. The shores were covered with a deep layer of ash, and vehicles couldn't move in the mush until bulldozers cleared paths. Over 7,000 tons of bombs, and almost as much tonnage from naval guns, rained on the island, but with little effect. It wasn't for lack of equipment that Iwo was a tough nut to crack. The invasion armada had close to 1,000 ships, including the small craft fleet of 500. The landing support force had six battleships, eight escort carriers, five cruisers, twenty destroyers and nine destroyer-escorts. The carrier task force was loaded with power, seventeen aircraft carriers, eight battleships, sixteen cruisers, and seventy-seven destroy-ers. The Marines had 110,000 men to draw from—the Japanese 20,000, and no chance of reinforcements. By March 26th the enemy was wiped out; there were only 200 survivors. The U.S. flag planted on top of Mt. Suribachi in February, in defiance of the enemy, a month later waved as a sign of victory. The Captain didn't interrupt the Major, as he instantly visualized war correspondent Joe Rosenthal's widely displayed immortal photograph of the six Marines raising the stars and stripes for the world to see. However, Iwo was costly, but necessary to gain the airstrip for emergency landings for the B-29s bombing Japan. The Air Force esti-mated there would be over 2,000 planes and 2,500 crewmen saved by having a safe place to set down on instead of the ocean.

The Major, by this time, was on his third mug and cigarette, and with no hesitation in his narrative. No doubt having an attentive listener and not another veteran was a pleasant change for him. He pointed out through the portlight Okinawa also was invulnerable to bombardment and as on Iwo, again the Japs were hidden in rock caves and tunnels and again they had to be driven out cave by cave. It was a regular Japanese Gibralter and it took until June 21st to capture it. As at Iwo, the U.S. put together a tremendous force of men and ships: 182,000 assault troops backed by 40 carriers, 18 battleships, 148 destroyers and destroyer-escorts along with support ships, landing craft and miscellaneous vessels totaling 1,400 and crewed by almost 500,000 men. However, the Japanese didn't give up. It was a suuicide stand to the finish, both on land and in the air—100,000 enemy troops went to their ancestors. Almost 8,000 Japanese planes were destroyed on the ground and in the air. It was reported the Japs produced 25,000 planes in 1944, but they were short of pilots. Up north of Okinawa, the 63,000-ton, 18″ gun, Japanese battleship *Yamoto*, was sunk by carrier planes. No doubt about it, the sun was rapidly setting in the land of the rising sun.

The Japanese had exacted a high price for the victory. The Major thought a moment, looked away, and then he continued. Apparently he didn't want to mention casualties, as he went right to ships. The *kamikazes* damaged thirteen carriers, ten battleships, five cruisers, ten battleships, five cruisers, eighty-eight destroyers and thirty destroyer-escorts. The suicide one-way planes came from hidden air bases, as many as 250 at a time, and they carried 1,000-pound bombs. There was no real defense against a pilot and plane coming at a ship intent on suicide and destruction. Some of the pilots were dressed in ceremonial *hari kiri* robes. Americans can't understand such tactics, such fanaticism— anyway, the Japs accomplished their purpose. They did the same things to the ships with their *Bakas*, the suicide projectile, and the one-man midget subs. No doubt there would have been more of the same on the next push if the big drop at Hiroshima on August 6th hadn't taken the fight out of them. Then the Nagasaki bomb ended all indecision. They realized that, when pressure waves from one bomb explosion flattened every building within two miles, there was a deadly power unleashed which they could never cope with. The Captain knew about Hiroshima, but not the details. The Major seemed very reluctant to talk about the bomb, so the Captain went back to the Okinawa conflict, and he asked if the Navy hospital ships handled the casualties. The answer was, "yes," because Iwo and Okinawa were largely Navy and Marine operations, but air lifts were also used to evacuate casualties. The Major looked at the chiming bulkhead clock, got up, accepted the Captain's offer to come back aboard for dinner and, after a handshake, headed for the accommodation ladder.

Unloading the 42nd's equipment from number three hatch finished on the 26th and the same day instructions came to proceed directly to Nojima Saki, Japan, for further orders, arriving August 30th. The *Marigold* now would be in position to witness the last act of the Pacific tragedy, the demise of the villain.

CHAPTER

XIX

After rounding Okinawa, the course was set directly for Nojima Saki at the end of the peninsula jutting out forty miles from Tokyo Bay. All the way north, speculation never ceased as to what the *Marigold* would do in Japan with operation "Coronet" scrubbed. Continue on to Seattle, return to Los Angeles, go back to Manila or Hollandia for a load of patients to the States, or become a passenger ship for returning high-pointers for discharge. Still, no one hit on the vital part the *Marigold* was to play in the occupation.

Traffic increased the closer the ship came to Nojima Saki, destroyers and destroyer-escorts in a hurry going and coming, but no heavy ships. The picket destroyer at the cape signalled to proceed to the station vessel five miles east of Yokohama breakwater. At 1200 hours, the ship was coming up to the command vessel when another destroyer issued a standby order. A motor launch came over and a Navy lieutenant, a Japanese naval officer and two sailors came aboard. The Lieutenant, friendly and in no hurry, informed the Captain the *Marigold* was to go alongside the north pier in Yokohama's inner harbor and the Japanese naval officer would pilot the ship clear of the entrance mine barrier. The mine field had not been swept and was still active. He also told the Captain the ship would be the first Allied vessel to enter Yokohama Harbor since the outbreak of the war, except for the destroyers.

After the Lieutenant explained the conduct to be observed ashore—side arms, no looting, no molesting—he gave the pilot a letter of instruction in Japanese and, with a second warning for the ship's personnel not to go ashore beyond the dock area, he and his two men left for their own ship.

The Captain ordered SLOW AHEAD on the engines, then turned to the pilot, pointed to the compass, and motioned in the direction of the harbor. The pilot apparently didn't intend using the compass and started motioning with his left and right hand to indicate which way to alter course. The pilot gave no indication he could understand English. After forty minutes, the Captain noticed a destroyer coming out of the harbor and the destroyer's course was over five hundred yards south of the *Marigold's!* The Captain tried, with pencil and paper and gestures, to locate the position of the mine field, but the pilot just shook his head. By now the Captain sensed something was wrong, stopped the ship, and hurried up to the flying bridge so he could see full circle and better control the ship to hold exact position until the destroyer answered his signal. It wasn't long in coming. The destroyer stopped, let out a siren blast, and signalled, "You are in the mine field; don't move ahead, don't anchor."

The Captain replied, "Pilot aboard suspect, will back out on exact reverse course, please advise when clear of field." The reply, "Back 500 yards, then move due south my position and follow." The "Wilco" was sent and the ship started astern. The Captain called down to the officers waiting in the bridge wing, "Cuff and handcuff the S.O.B.!" The three officers grabbed the pilot, booted him along to a stanchion, stretched his arms around the post and snapped on the irons. Much shouting on both sides accompanied the manhandling and the Japanese kept up what must have been strong language until properly silenced. After safely traveling thousands of hazardous miles and then, with hostilities over, to have the ship blown up by a saboteur was enough to bring on violent reactions.

With the ship in imminent danger, the Captain quickly decided to use the telephone in the engine room in order to get immediate response from the engines, either to increase or decrease the engine turns as needed to counteract any tendency of the ship to swing. Backing for five minutes in a straight line and the ship was clear. The space between mines was just right to allow the ship to slide through. The Captain later saw a plan of the mine field, and if the ship had gone another fifty yards, the change in spacing would have placed mines right in line with the ship's approach! At a signal from the destroyer, the *Marigold* headed for her new pilot and followed the destroyer through the breakwater. Once inside the inner harbor the danger was over and the ship swung to the right and headed for the north pier. For the first time in an hour, the Captain could think and act in a normal manner. The nightmare was over; only the thanksgiving remained.

No one showed up to take the tie-up lines, so four of the deck crew climbed down a pilot ladder and ran the eight-inch manila lines to the pier cleats. The destroyer waited until the *Marigold* was fast alongside, then sent a motorsailer and six men over to take the pilot in custody. He was kept locked up until the Japanese were able to re-establish their own law-and-order and deal with subversives and violators of the surrender agreement.

Was Yokohama a ghost town? Not a sound could be heard coming from the city; all was quiet as a graveyard, the area completely deserted. The Captain, with a group of staff and ship officers, walked up the pier to the port buildings to make sure there would be no unwelcome visitors during the night. Port piers and buildings were intact and, looking around the whole foreshore, it appeared the bombers had spared all the harbor facilities. But in back of the shoreside structures the industrial areas were leveled, though the residential sections on the hills overlooking the city seemed to be untouched. Not a soul could be found in or around the buildings and offices. Warehouses were bare except for discarded pieces of equipment. Satisfied, the party returned to the ship and elaborated on the desolate conditions ashore.

But two days after the *Marigold*'s arrival, the townspeople started to return. Many carried heavy, high bundles on their backs and shoved push-carts loaded with household goods. Yokohama suddenly came to life.

The Japanese citizens, largely women, children and old men, explained to the complement that the city was deserted for fear of being massacred by American barbarians! The *Marigold*'s people looked friendly, so the Japanese confided that they were relieved to see that the propaganda spread by the military rulers was untrue and they could walk the streets without fear for their lives.

Not a soldier, as such, had been spotted since arrival; what few had been in the area discarded their ragged uniforms and instantly became plain citizens. Actually, they had little to fight with and little food and, most of all, nothing to fight for. Few, if any, on the Allied side realized the true impoverished and defeated state of Japan. The ability and policy of the Japanese military leaders to continue senseless fighting on the outlying islands was misleading in relation to the hopeless and destitute conditions in the home islands. Surrender should have come before Iwo, before Okinawa, before Hiroshima and Nagasaki. Emperor Hirohito realized the futility and tragedy of continuing, but the war lords of the Imperial Council wouldn't agree, so the Emperor, in desperation, finally took action on his own—the cease-fire of August 14th. The *Marigold* personnel were among the first to hear from the returning populace of the ruthlessness and the stubbornness of the militant dictators. They were actually responsible for the unconscionable holocaust resulting from the two fission bombs. Early reports had indicated 330,000 killed, 230,000 wounded, 5,000 acres burned out, 85,000 buildings destroyed. The chief steward and two of the doctors were shown air force pictures of what was left of Hiroshima and, after viewing the annihilation, they thought the reported figures were no doubt true. It wasn't warfare, it was extermination. In the hands of the godless, the unholy device could be cataclysmic.

The *Marigold*'s preparatory rest period was now over. On the fourth day, orders were received to shift across the harbor on the following morning to the south pier, located by the harbormaster's office. The *Marigold* was about to engage in the most important work of her career. The question engaging everyone's mind was answered. The ship was to act as a station hospital for released POWs—starting the next afternoon and continuing until all were treated and ready for travel. To dispense tender loving care would be the order of the day.

Again, waiting to begin was a trial of patience, but an unwanted diversion came to make the time go faster. During the afternoon, a moderate breeze turned into a gale and, by evening, the wind was howling and gusting to thirty knots. At 2000 hours, an LST started out from the center pier across the harbor to Pier 3. The LST, slab-sided, couldn't hold up and was being driven by the wind more sideways than ahead and right for the *Marigold*! Unable to anchor and out of control, the LST signalled the *Marigold* to prepare for a crash. Fenders were hurriedly put over the side and the LST was asked to hold a broadside position relative to the *Marigold* to spread the impact. She just managed to hit broadside. The jolt sent a shock through the hull, but no damage resulted, though there were some pointed comments on the poor way to make a call.

The LST was wind-bound alongside until morning and, in discussing Leyte, her commanding officer told the Captain they were in on the December 7th landing at Ormoc Bay, Leyte, and in just two weeks Ormoc belonged to the Army. Controlling the Bay was important to stop the Japs from landing reinforcements for their armies in central Leyte. The Air Force stopped all troop landings to the point where the Japs had to bring in reinforcements by sailboats at night!

Next morning when working away from Pier 7, a Japanese tug—pulling the *Marigold*'s stern into the clear—parted her towing line, and the ship's starboard propeller wound the end around the hub, necessitating a diver to cut out the line. The *Marigold*'s hawser was used on the next pull; the tug's line was no doubt pre-war. In spite of the delay, the *Marigold* was tied up by 1100 hours alongside the south pier, gangway out and ready for the VIPs—very important patients.

The first four POWs arrived in an Army ambulance right at noon. All were men, emaciated, hunched over and wearing new army fatigues, but sizes too large. Looking up at the smiling faces along the rail, they smiled back, but the reaction came slowly, they had forgotten how, but interiorly they were overcome with joy to be free of their oppressors. Eight more loads came in the afternoon. The ambulances and jeeps were following all the roads they could find and picking up POWs along the way. The prisoners from the immediate area were turned loose by the Japanese and it was up to the men to find their way out. But those working in mines and from other distant camps came by plane and bus and many needed help to get aboard. The Japanese apparently were not partial who they put in their prison camps as many different nationalities came to the *Marigold* for help, though Americans predominated.

The processing was lengthy and thorough, including case history, treatments received, known disabilities, and a physical examination. Then, most important, rehabilitation started and continued until the patients were in condition to travel by air to a transfer station, then on to their home country. The ship's Red Cross office performed a valuable service for the patients by notifying relatives of their release, location and homecoming—the POW's greatest anxiety seemed to be to get word home.

As the hospital operated on a shift basis, there was time for trips ashore and several of the medics found a quick way to make a fast buck on their very first jaunt to the city. By now many of the shops were back in business and the banks had opened their doors. Noticing this, the four *Marigold* medics who collected Japanese occupation money in Manila had an inspiration. They rushed back to the ship and, with the bundles of money, headed for the biggest bank. Placing the stack on the counter and an American five-dollar bill alongside, they motioned from one to the other. The bank officer, unsmiling, said he understood English, so the transaction was simplified. Without hesitating, the Japanese counted the money in the four bundles, went in another room and, in a matter of minutes, came back with a handful of American bills. As he counted it out, the eyes of the four boys opened wider and wider. The officer handed them $1,600! The GIs, thinking a bow would be effective, bent from the waist, but only slightly, to impress the Japanese of their importance, then they made an unhurried exit.

The story of the new bonanza rapidly spread, and even pilots flying between Japan and the Philippines started bringing back money and presenting it for exchange. However, in less than a week, the banks refused to honor the money. At the beginning, the bankers were deathly afraid not to convert the money, but they stopped upon the advice and the orders of the U.S. Army officers administrating the occupation. The *Marigold* medics were excited about the easy money, but claimed they had more satisfaction from knowing they had exacted a little reparation from the Japanese.

Besides the POWs, others in need of medical attention were sent to the *Marigold*. Generals, Admirals, all ranks down the line, internees, even Tokyo Rose incognito. Rear Admiral Richard Byrd, visited by Admiral Spraunce and Vice-Admiral Wilkinson, came aboard for treatment of a heart condition. The staff also treated the highest-ranking general of the Japanese Army, who hadn't been successful in committing suicide, but hanging him along with General Yamashita, in December, as a war criminal was successful. With the ship operating as a peace-time station hospital, no distinction was made in race, creed or previous service—a true Hippocratic ship. The *Marigold*'s complement didn't complain about the new status—they were sympathic to anyone's troubles—the American way.

Cardinal Spellman from New York came to the ship to express the government's appreciation—in the form of material help and citations—for the sacrifices made by the POWs in the nation's cause. The Cardinal also offered a mass on the apron of the pier for the benefit of the POWs. They filled the ship's rails and, with many of the ship's personnel, followed the Mass part by part. Realizing the Cardinal came all the way from New York to be with them did wonders for the patients' morale.

All of the complement, the crew and, surprisingly, some of the POWs wanted souvenirs of Japan to take home, so Japanese dealers in pearls, carved ivory, silver trinkets, inlaid boxes, cinnabar boxes, cloisonné, and stone chinaware were allowed aboard. It was convenient for the patients and for the personnel. It saved traveling through littered, smelly, crowded streets. Cigarettes, as in Manila, had a good trading value along with American money, but sugar would buy anything. The Captain was offered six strings of bright butter-yellow cultured pearls for one sack of sugar. The only obstacle was that the government owned the sugar and what would the government do with six strands of pearls? A choker of green-black pearls was available for two sacks of flour. Food, food, food was the crying need. Kimonos that had taken a year to make were offered for canned fruit. Survival was a constant struggle.

Some of the staff had a first-hand view of the desperate struggle for survival when they were given helicopter trips over the twenty-mile stretch between Yokohama and Tokyo. They reported miles of twisted sheet metal, burned and rusted, people living in crude tin shacks. The B–29s, over 300 to the strike, had leveled the countryside. Half of Tokyo was a heap of rubble, but it was only one of sixty-four cities bombed out—the Japanese were faced with famine. When the Americans arrived, they put enmities aside to bring material relief to the Japanese people—and yet the gun barrels had scarcely cooled..

The formal surrender papers were signed September 2, 1945 on the battleship *Missouri*, with General MacArthur and Japanese Foreign Minister Shigemitsu the principal signers. Right after the surrender, General MacArthur as Supreme Commander of the Allied Powers, started a program of rehabilitation and reorganization, under Allied control and supervision, but disallowing any future build-up in military strength. Before the *Marigold* departed, Japan's destitute condition had noticeably improved—the defender unhesitantly healing the wounds of the aggressor.

The influx of POWs to the *Marigold* never slackened all through September and the staff became very adept at instantly recognizing the ailments peculiar to POWs: beriberi, dropsy, pellagra, scurvy, inflammations, worms and prison-camp neurosis. Beriberi—the most common affliction, caused by lack of vitamin B–1—brought on inflammation of the nerves and wasting away of the muscles, very evident in the men who had been in prison camps over a year.The doctors classed some of the advanced cases as "wet beriberi," when edema (dropsical swelling) was present. The dropsy patients were always put to bed and their strength built up with proper diet and vitamins. A prison fare of rice and grasshoppers was hardly conducive to good health.

Pellagra—another of their deficiency diseases (lack of niacin)—appeared, but not as general as beriberi. The POWs suffering from mental disturbances were non-violent and, with the change in environment and with affection replacing abuse, they were assured of returning to a normal, stable condition. The patients afflicted with scurvy (lack of vitamin C and fresh foods) showed distinct signs of weakness, pain in the legs, bleeding gums and purple patches in the skin from bleeding under the skin. The same treatment was given to relieve scurvy as the other deficiency diseases. Usually the POWs suffered from more than one condition. However, the same general treatment benefited all the deficiencies. It is a wonder they survived from their description of long hours of forced work, physical abuse from whippings done for exercise by the guards, kicks, blows and standing at attention for long periods. Martyrs in the cause of their country.

One of the patients, a British nurse captured in Singapore early in the war and a POW in Japan, told the staff of a heart-rending experience she went through just a few months past. She developed a tumor and bleeding so she knew surgery had to be done. The American prison doctor whom she worked with seemed to know his business and he recommended a complete hysterectomy. The only difficulty—the prison had no anesthetics. She waited as long as possible, then decided to go through with the operation using whiskey for courage and a pain-killer.

An agonizing two-hour-long ordeal and the surgery was done, but the pain continued for days. She recovered, though she said the pain and mental stress would never be forgotten. A devout woman, she said the Lord gave her the grace of tolerance and strength and she made many acts of thanksgiving. She was treated with the greatest respect and admiration by the staff. She left the ship for England with a heavy purse and a light heart but she left behind an example of profound courage.

The POWs continued to come until the middle of October; then, except for bed patients, the *Marigold* hospital only treated cases from the shore establishment. When the first Army shore hospital would be ready for operation, the Army's floating hospital would be released and free to go about the business of transporting patients.

But before leaving Japan—so the ship would appreciate the many and long periods of calm weather—the fringe of a typhoon struck Yokohama Harbor and the *Marigold.* However, a warning was received in time to take necessary precautions—lines were doubled, steam raised to operate the main engines and the windlass made ready for letting go anchors. The wind hit at 1900 hours forcing the ship away from the pier. The anemometer read sixty knots. Lines tightened like fiddle strings, drops of water squeezed out of the strands. The wind whistled around the deckhouses and in the rigging making an eerie whine, the pitch rising as gusts reached eighty knots. Then, thirty minutes later, the gauge read a steady seventy. The lines were surged to keep from breaking, but even so two parted and flew through the air like whips.

The marine-wire lines were not strong enough to hold the ship so the Captain dropped both anchors and worked the port engine astern to help hold the stern in. The wire spring-line leading forward took the backing pull of the propeller. A rock bulkhead 200 feet off the port side prompted the Captain to ease the stern a little farther from the pier so the starboard engine could be safely worked ahead. The combination held the ship in position for four hours, then the wind slacked and dropped to twenty knots. At daylight, only a breeze remained. Heavy rain fell before the wind gained strength, then ceased altogether—a fortunate circumstance as the visibility remained unimpaired. The old sailing ship axiom again proved true: "If the rain before the wind, your topsails you should mind."

All the portlights had been secured as soon as the warning came, making the wards snug and quiet. The patients knew nothing of the strength of the storm so they were not concerned. Since most of the POWs were still jittery, every effort was made and at all times to keep the ship quiet and tranquil.

Word came from the new Port Commander, General Duke, from Charleston, that the ship was to leave for Manila with passengers on

November 10th, and from there on the future would be in the hands of the port surgeon in Manila. November 10th would make the seventieth day of the *Marigold*'s stay in Japan and, if not another hospital bed was ever occupied, treating and nurturing the POWs made the *Marigold*'s existence—her reason for being—totally worthwhile. And for the satisfaction of the Women's Clubs in Seattle, by their helping hand to the *Marigold* they had extended a helping hand to the long-suffering POWs.

A week beore departure the Captain came down with atypical pneumonia, diagnosed by Dr. (Captain) Gaynes, and hospitalized at his direction. Not having far to go to a hospital, the Captain reported to Lieutenant Mary Stypul's ward in minutes and she lodged him in one of her semi-private rooms. It was the first time for him in a hospital bed and the first time a girl ever ordered him to slip down his pajamas. The Captain was sure from the too-wide smile that Mary was going to get a kick out of doing her thing. She quickly jabbed the penicillin needle in the muscle and quickly emptied it so he could enjoy the burning sensation. There wasn't any particular reason, it was just an opportunity to have command of the commander. But one hot-shot needling was enough to show who was boss and, after establishing control, Mary was a most attentive and considerate nurse and she, along with Ollie Kneubel, had the Captain back topside in time to sail the ship.

CHAPTER

XX

On November 9th the patients for Manila came aboard. All were ambulatory, although the Dutch group looked as if they should be carried. They had been through a prolonged ordeal, being interned since the Japanese seizure of the Dutch East Indies early in the war. Other than patients, there were 300 able-bodied passengers, largely military, on their way to eventual discharge in the States.

Next morning, as the 1000-hour sailing time approached, more and more people came down the pier, some military, but mostly Japanese of all ages. Girls in bright kimonos wearing high hair styles with fancy combs were out in force. From the smiles and the bows, they didn't come down just out of curiosity—they had acquaintances aboard—the waving from the deck proved they did. To most of the Japanese, the presence of the big white ship with the red crosses had become a symbol of peace, hope and help, so they came to pay their respects. They actually appeared to be saddened by the departure. From now on, there would be only gray ships to look at, with a different significance. To recognize the gestures of *"bon voyage"*, the Captain sounded three whistles as the ship pulled away from the berth. The Japanese congregated at the end of the pier and waved little white flags with a painted red cross in the center. It was their way of expressing gratitude to the flag of goodwill.

This time, going through the entrance, there was nothing to fear. The minesweepers had long since swept the way. No Navy clearance or briefing was necessary since all the Japanese submarines with die-hard commanders had been rounded up and there were no Japanese combat surface ships at sea; 98% of the Imperial Fleet rested on the bottom. However, the danger of striking detached mines drifting in the sea lanes was as much a threat as ever and would be for a long time. The watch officers on the bridge were warned to be especially alert because the route to Manila ran close to mined areas in former combat zones.

On the third day out, a black floating object was reported a point off the bow and a mile away. In another two minutes, the floating object turned out to be a mine! Word spread quickly of the presence, and the complement's Warrant Officer hurried up to the bridge and asked permission to try and sink the mine with rifle fire. He explained the rifle had been given to him in Leyte! The Captain quickly thought this would be a chance to uncover the guns he suspected were hidden on the ship and couldn't be located. He agreed to stop the ship and give the rifle a chance, but at a safe distance, in case the mine exploded. Knowing the short effective range of the thirty-calibre carbines, the Captain held the ship far enough off for the bullets to fall short but at the same time accomplish his purpose, to bring out all the rifles aboard the ship for a try at the mine. Ten appeared and fired a clip, of course without effect. The Captain requested all the sharpshooters to deliver their guns to the Sergeant-Major for safe-keeping. Even if the war was over, firearms in the hands of ship personnel could be dangerous, especially if they were used to settle arguments. The Captain intended to inform the potential gun-smugglers that, if they were caught possessing government rifles, it could cost them $5,000 and five years—hardly worth it, even for a souvenir that helped thin the ranks of the Japanese Army.

Two round black net-floats were sighted, but no more mines. However, the ship passed flotsam and jetsam all the way south. Two unoccupied rubber rafts with clothes and life jackets, galvanized boat tanks, barrels, gratings, hatch covers, logs, and masses of kelp, but no sign of human life except on the many ships passing northbound, hurrying supplies to Japan.

In Bashi Channel, north of Luzon, a Liberty ship coming up close started signalling. To everyone's amazement on the bridge, the ship turned out to be their old friend from Leyte burdened with 5,000 tons of bombs. He had good news; he had finally peddled the eggs in Manila and gone back to San Francisco for another cargo—this time it was beer—and, believe it or not, he was having a time getting rid of it, but he wasn't worried. It wouldn't blow him sky high. The captain of the Liberty sent thanks for being so friendly, gave three whistles and pulled away. This time the *Marigold's* crew did the cap-waving—concern about the survival of the Liberty's crew was over.

On November 17th, the anchor again splashed into Manila Bay and, knowing when the ship would arrive, the officers from the port surgeon's office were waiting. Eagerly coming over the rail, they blurted right out to the Colonel and the Captain, waiting to greet them, "You're going to be home for Christmas!" The ship would dock the next day, discharge passengers, and the following day load patients and passengers for Los Angeles, sailing November 20th—back to the States, home for Christmas! Bearers of such glad tidings deserved a special kind of thanks and they all headed for the Colonel's cabin.

Next morning, as soon as the pier gangway was secured in the side port, a friend of the Captain's from Seattle, Major Plott Medford, came aboard and invited the Captain and guests for a trip to Corregidor. Twelve of the ship's personnel were eager to go, including five nurses who had cared for Santo Tomas-Corregidor patients on the last trip. The Major's fast army motor launch landed the party on the island at San Jose, making the twenty-six-mile run in an hour. An Army sergeant stationed on the island was assigned to guide the party through the interior maze of passageways. Without a guide to lead the way out, they would have missed the *Marigold's* sailing! Inside the island, alleyways, side tunnels, subways, all blasted out of solid rock, led in every direction. They were poorly lighted and some had tracks on the rock floor. Huge caverns for storing shells and supplies were numerous. The heavy artillery guns at the open end of the firing tunnels were all upset and shattered by naval gunfire. The sergeant said it took a whole month and continuous firing by the Navy destroyers, shooting right into the gun tunnels, to silence the batteries once and for all. But the fight didn't end until the defenders blew themselves up in the tunnels. Later, a total of 4,215 dead Japanese were counted. With the victory, the marine highway to Manila was again safe to travel. To the *Marigold* group—as rank odors and a feeling of depression emanated from all the corridors—an hour of exploring was quite enough.

The Major's boat next ran the group over to Mariveles, at the end of the Bataan Peninsula, six miles from Corregidor, and everyone went ashore and made short work of the food prepared by the *Marigold's* pantryman. While having lunch, the Major described the struggle to hold Bataan that ended in the infamous Bataan March, forced on surrendered American and Filipino troops, driving them like cattle to prison camps in Manila.

He started by saying the Japs landed in Lingayen Gulf December 22nd, 1941 with 60,000 troops. They also made landings on the Luzon coast and they controlled the sea and approaches. At the same time, the Japs heavily bombed Manila, inflicting a heavy loss of life. So, on December 26th, General MacArthur declared Manila an open city and moved his headquarters to Corregidor. In January the Japs invaded Mariveles, but time and again were driven back by Filipino scout troops until Tojo sent in overpowering forces. The main American and Filipino troops were concentrated on a defending line across the center of the

Bataan Peninsula, but by March they were forced back by massive attacks and bombing. The defenders put up unbelievable resistance considering their hardships. There was no way to get help or food to them and they faced starvation. They were on half rations for a month and then the half was cut in half. Not only the Major, but also his intent listeners shook their heads at every astonishing fact. The Major seemed to do a little editing as he went along, probably to skip some of the more grisly details.

By April, the troops hadn't the strength to carry on and, on April 9th, General King surrendered and the Bataan March started in the blazing sun. Brutally, the exhausted troops were forced to march. Hundreds died on the way and thousands more died as a result of the march and from later mistreatment, the whole episode one of the great calamities of the war.

Any comment would be anti-climactic, so the Captain asked about General MacArthur. President Roosevelt ordered the General to Australia to assume command of the entire Pacific defense. He and his party left on March 12th, 1942 by motor torpedo boat to Mindanao, then on by B–17 bomber. General Wainwright assumed command on Corregidor and held out for two months against the Japanese assault of bombers, naval rifles and the never-ending waves of troops. It was another case of exhaustion, starvation and no chance for relief, so Corregidor fell to the enemy on May 5, 1942. A disaster that never should have happened. The Major must have felt quite bitter about the events as he stood up at his last remark and just motioned everyone to the boat.

By the time the motor launch had returned the Major's guests to the ship, all the Yokohama passengers were on their way to either the Manila Hotel, the staging area, the Army hospital, MATS airport (Military Air Transport Service) or re-established consular offices. And for the *Marigold*, it would be two more nights in Manila, twenty-one nights on the Pacific, then Point Fermin and the Wilmington pier, the gateway to the future.

To four of the *Marigold*'s personnel, the future suddenly took on a new and thrilling meaning. Dan Symmes, the second steward, married Captain Gladys Saterbak, the chief nurse, and medic Sergeant Spencer married Lieutenant Lucille Lakin. Both couples wanted to be married in Manila so the weddings took place ashore. Their secret romances were very private affairs, as the outcome was a surprise, but a pleasant one. The *Marigold* provided the opportunity and the Army provided the partners. However, their aboard-ship roommates would be the same as they always had. There were no "honeymoon" suites on the *Marigold*, but love always finds a way.

CHAPTER

XXI

Trans-Pacific passengers and patients started arriving mid-morning November 19th and by late afternoon every berth was occupied. The entire University of Maryland Hospital Unit came aboard, returning home after three years in the Pacific theatre. They looked wan and care-worn, but understandably so, after months in the debilitating climate of the New Guinea jungle and later enduring the monotony and perils of the coast ports.

Only half the passenger list were patients; the rest simply required passage, not care. Army, Navy, Marine Corps, Coast Guard, Nurse Corps, WACS, Red Cross, USO, Merchant Marine—all were represented. With everyone in the same frame of mind and having the same end in view— discharge—the voyage would be a happy one—and, for the weary, recuperative—enhancing the joy of their homecoming. By 1000 hours on the 20th, Manila had passed from view and there wasn't a tear in sight.

A helicopter enlivened the run down to Corregidor, catching the ship, hovering over the after-hatch and dropping down a yellow-colored package on a weighted line. Two of the deck crew detached the small square bundle. Up went the line and, with what looked like clasped hands waving at the window, the copter slid off sideways and headed for Manila.

The address on the package read, "Please deliver to 1st Lieutenant Mary Kelly, U.S. Army Nurse Corps, passenger, Hospital Ship *Marigold*. Thanks." No return address given. The package was promptly delivered, but it took a week of coaxing before the Lieutenant would reveal the contents of the package wrapped in waterproofed silk. The helicopter pilot, a Captain, was her ardent suitor whenever the Army gave him the time and the package contained her ID tag and chain, a hotel room key, a red rose, and his class ring. The whole story, past present and future in four tokens. It must have had a happy ending.

This time, instead of continuing north from Cape Bojeador, the ship swung east through Babuyan Channel along the north coast of Luzon, then headed a little north of east for Marcus Island, 2,100 miles away. The island would make a good check on the accuracy of the navigation before the long haul, 4,400 miles to Los Angeles. Marcus, only a small volcanic island about a mile square, would not be an interesting sight except to the navigators. However, it was a former Japanese supply base. A week's run should bring the island abeam, but the distance made each day would be influenced by an adverse current causing a loss of five to seven miles every twenty-four hours.

Thanksgiving Day and Marcus came at the same time, with the day far more important than the island. The Chaplains held a combined service on the foredeck and they didn't have to try hard to create a feeling of thanksgiving what with the war and all its struggles over and the ship headed for home. Thanksgiving was in everyone's heart. Just to mention the word "home" and its meaning of love, peace, safety, happiness, brought a sense of well-being and an appreciation of the sacrifices that made it possible. Chaplain Lanning's talk closed with some inspired words. "What we have witnessed these past months will fade away but we shouldn't ever forget the meaning of Pearl Harbor, the Turkey Shoot, the Bataan March, St. Tropez, Corregidor, Iwo, Okinawa—the POWs and all the tragedies—ours and our enemies. We who have been there have to make sure that nobody will ever be forced to learn the tragic lesson all over again." The Chaplain ended the service with a prayer to remember this day forever. During the service, high fleecy clouds covered the western sky, then just as the prayer started, the sun broke through and everyone looked up. If there was a significance, it wasn't lost.

Weather-wise, the voyage was turning out to be a duplicate of the last one to Los Angeles, fine and calm with scattered cotton-ball-like clouds, but this time no Makin Atoll rain squalls appeared to wash down the ship. The *Marigold's* unbroken record of storm-free passages when patients were aboard might very well remain intact. So far so good, and Marcus only hours away.

Just before sighting the island, the Captain remembered having heard about some sort of naval action at Marcus, from the tanker captain at Manus. He recalled some of the story for the *Portholer*, but the paper asked for more, hoping someone aboard would know all that had happened. A chief petty officer did. He had been assigned to the destroyer *Fanning* shortly after the engagement, so he knew what had happened.

He said the High Command had selected Marcus to draw Japanese attention from larger forces which were aiming to strike Iwo and

Okinawa, with a secondary objective of the Marcus mission to destroy the radio and weather station, supply dumps and buildings. On October 9th, 1944 three cruisers firing six- and eight-inch shells and six destroyers firing five-inch shells bombarded the island on three sides. The Japanese shore batteries returned the fire, but with little effect. Before attacking, the Task Force released balloons carrying radar reflectors to show on the Japanese radar screens to give the impression of a large force of ships involved. At night they also put out lights on floats to simulate ships. Of course the ships were far enough away in the daytime so they couldn't be counted. Whether the diversion part of the attack accomplished the purpose couldn't be determined, but shelling the island out of commission was completely successsful.

Again, as at Kwajelein, passing Marcus and knowing it had been demolished and now rebuilt and usable was hard to believe, but gratifying to see the physical evidence of American ingenuity. Marcus had appeared three points off the bow as predicted, so the ship was making her course good and the navigators were pleased that their position-plotting had proved correct.

The next point of consequence, the International Date Line, 1,300 miles away, required having two days of the same date, and for the crew Sundays would be preferred. The two days did turn out to be Sundays. However, there was only one Sunday religious service with Chaplain Lanning directing group singing on the foredeck—hymns and ending with songs typical of America. With only piano accompaniment, the 200-strong voices singing in unusual unison and easily heard all over the ship touched an appreciative and sentimental audience. It was unforgettable.

Outside of movies, Chaplain Lanning didn't attempt planned entertainment. It wasn't necessary with the prevailing feeling of contentment throughout the ship. The passengers were satisfied to just relax on deck with their thoughts centered far to the east. Diversion was not important, but planning for the future was, now that time would soon be their own. The days didn't drag, they weren't impatient ones, but the last 3,200 miles from Midway Island to Los Angeles would no doubt seem never-ending.

Midway Island, 1,600 miles from Marcus and part of the Hawaiian chain, could not be seen with the course line 180 miles to the north, but even so the ship passed through the area of the battle of Midway (June 3–6, 1942) where the Japanese Navy was lambasted to teach them the error of their ways. As the battle was so crucial, Captain Mieczkowski volunteered to give the *Portholer* what information he had collected. He probably had some personal interest in the battle, but didn't say so.

At Midway, the Japanese rush to take over the whole Pacific was stopped, the battle turned the tide, it was critical and decisive, putting Japan on the defensive. Midway was a long range air engagement entailing no surface combat. The planes came from carriers with some help from land-based bombers and fighters based at Midway. The U.S. could put together a defensive force of only three carriers, eight cruisers, sixteen destroyers and a few auxiliaries against the Japanese offensive forces of ten battleships, five carriers, eighteen cruisers, fifty-seven destroyers, three seaplane tenders and seven auxiliaries, a total of one hundred ships against thirty-three of the U.S.! The Japanese had the advantage of numbers but, warned of the Japanese advance, the U.S. had the advantage of surprise. They sent out planes to intercept at 200 miles and they singled out the carriers as the heart of the fleet and bombed four of them right out of existence. That was enough for the Japs, they turned and ran wanting no more of that kind of treatment, but before they got away one cruiser was sunk and one severely damaged. The Japs lost 3,500 men and 250 planes. The U.S. lost the big carrier *Yorktown*, one destroyer, and 150 planes. A small price to pay to turn back an overwhelming force that could have done irreparable damage had they kept coming.

The lack of tools to fight with created formidable battle odds in favor of the enemy and had sadly prolonged the war to almost four years. George Washington's legacy—"To preserve peace, be prepared for war"—had been ignored. Months and months of intensive production were required to correct the imbalance as Japan had been making obvious preparations for years and not for defense. The Armed Forces' skill and strategy could offset only so much politically ignored enemy superiority in armament and position—praiseworthy military action and censurable political inaction.

With the battle for peace resolved, it was time to settle the battle of cards waged aboard the *Marigold*. Four of the doctors had played bridge off and on for a year and a half and they decided that, with the end of the voyage only eleven days away, they should end the game and post the score in the *Portholer*. After 400 rubbers the difference was only 400 points! The inference appeared to be that, if the game were played long enough, the difference between the winners' and the losers' scores would be small. The paper commented that the players' abilities and luck would have to be similar, or the law of averages wouldn't work.

Logically the *Portholer* had become a second oracle at Delphi and manager of all special events, including a staff popularity poll. However, with the press of work in getting out the homecoming edition, the results were delayed, but nonetheless valid. The top eight received more congratulations than votes—sixty votes and twice as many hand-shakes.

For the nurses—Kathryn Adams was acclaimed the most appealing, Mary Donohoe the most cheerful, June Connell the most comely, and Mary Morehead the most desirable.

On the masculine side—the most handsome turned out to be Donn Stewart, the most professional Leonard Gaynes, the most entertaining Paul Jones, and the most serious was a tie between Kenneth Beebe and Harry Petard.

The result would have been the same any time in the past twenty months—a compliment to each one.

For prizes, they each received a key-ring pendant or dangle made of colored silk cords fashioned by Chief Officer Ray Fosse into a small, square, four-strand, Turk's-head knot with a coxcomb chain—unique and intended as a keepsake.

The *Portholer* also published a list of the service awards that applied to the whole complement and approved for the *Marigold*, so the personnel would know what ribbons they were entitled to wear:

> The American Theatre Campaign Medal
> The Europe-Africa-Middle East Campaign Medal
> Battlestar for the Rome-Arno Campaign
> Battlestar for the Invasion of Southern France
> The Asiatic-Pacific Campaign Medal
> Battlestar for the Luzon Campaign
> Battlestar for the Leyte Campaign
> Battlestar for the New Guinea Campaign
> Battlestar for the Western Pacific Campaign
> The Philippine Liberation Medal
> The Good Conduct Medal
> The Medal for Service in World War II
> The Meritorious Service Unit Award
> The Bronze Star

In the final issue, the *Portholer* listed some interesting *Marigold* facts for everyone's diary: Over 75,000 accident-free miles sailed on the various missions. Crossed the equator fourteen times. Total fuel consumption, 217,000 barrels. Ten thousand patients hospitalized. First hospital ship to operate as a complete general hospital and first Army hospital ship in the South Pacific. Very important accomplishments—2,000 POWs given *Marigold* care. Special blessing—always calm weather when patients were aboard. Everything considered, she deserved a medal, an illustrious medal, the Distinguished Service Medal.

The *Portholer* had asked the Captain to write a comment on the miles of safe voyaging as an ending to the paper's recounting of the ship's facts, and he did. "In the *Marigold's* logbook drawing to a close with the war over, there were incidents, events, accomplishments, successes, trials, dangers, problems and excitement. But there were no costly adventures. A seven-ocean sailor once wrote, 'Adventures result from lack of preparation or taking undue chances'."—words that *Marigold* took to heart.

During the last few days of the voyage, gatherings in the lounge became more frequent for the staff and the sessions lasted longer than in the past when there was always another day to look forward to. Recounting *Marigold* days from Seattle to Los Angeles via way-ports was the favorite subject. And whenever the Captain stopped by the lounge, he liked most to hear the staff's comments on ship life and the "I remember" stories, especially when the ship had a part.

The story of the Japanese fireman that came aboard accompanied by his mother and wanting to learn how to perform surgery in one quick lesson was the staff's favorite. The man, with the best of intentions, wanted to change his profession and help his people as there were so few doctors. He wanted the *Marigold's* surgeons to help him remove his mother's appendix (appendectomies were in most demand, so he said). He asked the surgeons to guide his hands and explain each move. He said he could do hypnosis so his mother would be relaxed and feel no pain and be able to translate directions and descriptions. She was an ex-school teacher and spoke very good English. Of course, the mother didn't have appendicitis. The man was told, through his mother, and in a most serious manner, that what he asked was strictly forbidden as it would be classed as experimental surgery. A look of keen disappointment came over the man's face, but he left thanking and bowing all the way to the door. The doctors had no end of enjoyment describing, with variations, how the whole operation would have been performed.

The Captain remembered the Japanese coming aboard, but not why. He told the doctors they were just simply afraid to do the job because they didn't know where the appendix was located in a Japanese. Which reminded the doctors to ask the Captain if he knew where mines were located in a Japanese harbor? That stopped the comments, but not the laughter.

When the two nurses chatting with Captain Mieczkowski left for the buffet table, the Captain walked over to the Chaplain and asked him how he happened to have so many facts on the Midway Battle. He either had a good memory or a good journal. The Captain had both to rely on. Smiling, the Chaplain said that when he visited the Army hospital in Manila he talked with patients that were a part of the Midway and Pearl

Harbor battles. He listened to their descriptions and their bitter comments on being caught with our guard down.

"You know, the Bible also has something to say about that very thing." The Captain looked a bit surprised, so the Chaplain quoted from memory a passage according to St. Luke, "—but of this be assured, that if the householder had known at what hour the thief was coming, he would certainly have watched and not have let his house be broken into." The Chaplain recalled another passage, "—when the strong man, fully armed, guards his courtyard, his property is undisturbed. But if a stronger than he attacks and overcomes him, he will take away all his weapons that he relied upon and will divide his spoils—" Then the Chaplain quickly added, "That's what the Lord said and we don't dare forget it again."

"Not if we expect to hold our own!" Both the Captain and the Chaplain after a moment's reflection looked more intently at the patriotic painting over the sideboard, Archibald Willard's "The Spirit of '76," presented to the ship at the same time as the sponsor's flag.

The Chaplain turned back to the Captain and his deliberate words left an indelible impression. "Few realize it. Life is warfare. Mankind has always had an unseen enemy to contend with—evil forces that find champions without number. We put down one set—another rises. There is no respite." Then he touched the picture. "This truly shows what it takes."

There was a thoughtful silence among the group that had gathered around. Then Helen Tipton, the dietician and one of the most avid readers aboard the ship remarked, "I couldn't help listening to you and an appropriate quote from James Russel Lowell occurred to me, 'If you want peace, the thing you've got to do is just to show you're up to fightin' too.'" The smiles and nods from everybody within range brought on more quotes, but shortly and as usual, the original subject changed to personalities.

The lounge continued to be a center for hail and farewell parties and farewell it would be for the original members of the complement headed for discharge and private life. The Colonel entertained his officers and some of the ship's officers in small groups in the lounge to exchange compliments, *Marigold* history, and the realities of civilian life. Now was the time on the last lap and with no inhibitions to acknowledge all the personal contributions to the harmony and success of the *Marigold* venture, for once ashore the unity, interdependence and ties of the past two years would be over.

One of the charge-nurses, Lieutenant Josephine Kaser, at the colonel's first party told of a touching incident apropos of what can happen in adjusting to civilian life. The Lieutenant started out by saying her family lived in the same block as a widow and her three children who were long-time friends. The oldest boy spent four years in the army just before the war and upon discharge hurried home. Later, he told his mother that he walked from the station, going slower and slower as he drew near his place. He walked right past and on around the block. Four times he made the circle, studying each house, small store, playfield, school, neighbors. His mother had witnessed the last three circuits, but did nothing, understanding the problem. During the four army years he didn't have to think for himself, his days were planned, he had no decisions to make, come what may payday always came, he was never alone. Now he suddenly became a detached individual with no definite aim, no sense of security and no settled future. He had to face up to problems he couldn't immediately resolve. Would the answer be to re-enlist? But walking and looking around the neighborhood forced him to think of events, school, athletics, friends, summer jobs—problems in all of them and all overcome. Then on the fifth time around he was able to open the gate and go in. His mother greeted him as only a mother can and, to make his smile full-blown, she said, "You know, coming back home you come back to love—the army can't give you that." Jo Kaser stopped, then went on, "I've never forgotten his mother's potent words." Everyone wanted more of the story, but she said, "The problem quickly disappeared, there isn't anymore to tell." After an unusually long lull, conversation started again, but on the upcoming farewell dinner and what could be done to enhance a spirit of thanksgiving.

Rather than have the farewell dinner the night before arrival with all the clean-up activity, the chief steward arranged to have it the last Sunday at sea. Even without a market close by, the menu was a revelation: grape juice, relish dishes, tomato soup aux croutons, baked Virginia ham and raisin sauce, roast Tom turkey, celery dressing, gravy, cranberry sauce, whipped potatoes, candied sweet potatoes, asparagus tips, buttered peas, hot Parker House rolls, hot mince pie, pumpkin pie, ice cream, American cheese, saltines, Oregon cream brick cheese, coffee, tea, cocoa—no one left the table hungry and some had a hard time leaving without trying all the dishes. The steward had given the tables a Thanksgiving Day appearance with drawings of medics as pilgrims and the *Marigold* as the *Mayflower*, finally landing at Plymouth Rock, all portraying the spirit of gratitude for coming through the hostilities unscathed.

After dinner the Captain and the Colonel sat in the Colonel's office for some memorable reminiscing. They were pleasant recollections because at their first meeting they agreed that unreserved cooperation for the ship's good would insure success and they never deviated from the policy. However, they recognized that each had a separate and distinct responsibility. The Captain to run the ship from port to port and the Colonel to run the hospital and care for the patients port to port. An hour of reminiscent traveling on the *Marigold* brought them back to longitude 128° west; it was time to knock-off. The colonel gave the Captain a firm handshake and "Thanks for the boat ride." The Captain, uniform cap on, answered, "May your hand always be steady, Colonel" and with a salute turned and stepped over the doorway coaming for the last time.

CHAPTER

XXII

With all the amenities discharged, the Captain spent the day before arrival finishing reports for the home office—the most important being for the Superintendent, Water Division, Los Angeles Port of Embarkation—a long voyage report, in the making for several days, covering six months of travel, events, ship operation, achievements and conclusions. The reports after each voyage were always carefully composed because they greatly influenced the ship's efficiency rating. The Captain found out later-on the newspapers published excerpts from his report, giving the most space to the POW section. The *Marigold* had made the papers for the fourth time. Office work being anathema to a sailor, the Captain was happy to be able to forget syntax and get back to thinking like a seaman.

On the May trip when approaching the San Pedro Islands, dense fog had closed off visibility until reaching San Nicolas Island, sixty miles from Los Angeles, but fortunately this time the weather held fine and clear, in deference no doubt to the final sea voyage on an Army ship for most of the passengers. With the ship passing through the same area where the fog had been thick enough to cut, the senior watch officer, Rex Harwood asked the Captain if he remembered the baffling fog signal that had everybody worried and guessing. The Captain nodded, then laughed, "How could I ever forget." The whole incident suddenly came alive.

Not far from the Cortes Bank, fishboats or sport fishermen were sounding foghorns and the Captain, as a precaution, cut the speed from half to slow. Suddenly a horn sounded close aboard and dead ahead. The telegraph handles went to STOP then to FULL ASTERN when the loud, piercing blast of a horn answered the ship's whistle. The bridge crew expected a collision any second as the horn still sounded right ahead. The only answer could be that a boat was traveling in the same direction; even so, their fog signal never changed position, but then, sound direction and distance in dense fog could be decptive.

The Captain, by now suspicious of the exchange of signals sent the junior officer and the lookout up to the forecastle head to investigate. The fog limited the visibility to a murkey ten feet. The two men were back on the bridge in minutes and between them a scared GI passenger hugging a bugle! The situation, serious but comic, prevented the soldier from an explosion of choice words from the Captain. So he let him off with a warning. The boy, a regular bugler, thought it would be fun to answer the ship's whistle and he, with two buddies, groped their way forward to play the game of tit-for-tat. He said he didn't realize he would cause a problem. He kept his bugle, but not his composure.

The Captain still smiling over the incident—it was named the bugler's bungle—went in to the chartroom to make another check on the accuracy of the ETA sent in seventy-two hours ahead of arrival. It still looked good and should be within a few minutes of 1500 hours. The Port's reply to the ETA stated that the walking passengers would debark in the afternoon, the litter patients the following morning.

For the ship's crew, all the goodbyes, good luck, best wishes, and good sailing had been said many times in the past few days, so only ship's business with the Port remained. Then the Captain and his officers would be ready for annual leave or, in some cases, to leave the service. The Captain's next move would be up to the Seattle Port of Embarkation since, before departing Manila, he had sent a letter asking whether he should return to Seattle for reassignment. The Army's transports would be operating for years as they had for the past seventy, but hospital ships, due to their nature, would operate only during national emergencies.

Approaching the Wilmington Pier, "Home Sweet Home" played by a uniformed band came over beautifully and from the looks on the passengers' faces lining the rail, effectively. No Hollywood entertainers were on hand this time, but the crowd was much larger, the outer half of the apron completely filled.

From the enthusiasm of the people on the pier they must have all been relatives or friends of the passengers. Between calls from the pier and shouts from onboard no one could understand a word or know where to look. An announcement from the ship quieted the hubbub somewhat. The able passengers would debark in twenty minutes and be first off, then the ambulatory patients, and they would remain on the pier for thirty minutes before leaving by bus. Relatives of litter patients could come aboard for one hour's visit after all others had debarked. This satisfied everybody and the band played for fifteen minutes more, then departed, waving back at the clasped-hands thank-you from the GIs at the rail.

The Port's Chief of Operations came up to the bridge, met the Captain, and they stepped into the quiet of the chartroom. Washington had sent orders to send the ship to San Francisco for lay-up and if the Captain did not want to wait around and make the delivery the Port would have one of their standby masters take the ship up. Before deciding, the Captain read the letter the Colonel had given him from the Seattle Port. Instructions were for the Captain to return to Seattle, go on leave, then report to the Kaiser Yard in Richmond, California and follow through on the conversion to Army specifications of a 12,000-ton transport the Navy turned back to the Army. The Captain was to bring the ship to Seattle and take command on a run to Japan, China and Korea, transporting Army personnel, dependents and civilian government employees. He thought as he read that from now on it would be passengers not patients, rough seas not light swells, blue coats not khaki shirts.

The Captain turned the letter over to the Colonel to read and then the Colonel volunteered to make all the transfer arrangements the next day. Before leaving, he invited the Captain to a meeting in the morning with the Superintendent.

A quiet night aboard was welcome after all the hustle of the past few days. The crew must have felt the same way; there was no sign or sound of activity around the upper decks. However, packing had to be done, difficult though it was. The Captain felt he was abandoning a family and home that had been nurtured and protected for years. If the break-up of the *Marigold* family had been due to economic causes rather than the end of the war, there would be many regrets, but under the circumstances the only regret from the dissolution was the loss of association with valued shipmates. The common cause that held them aboard in close rapport no longer existed; they were about to become individuals again with individual aims and new associates.

At the morning meeting, the Superintendent, Colonel Merchant, was keenly interested in the events of the *Marigold* since leaving the Port in July and afterward he presented the Captain with a complimentary letter and a copy of a letter to the Seattle Port advising of the lay-up plans for the *Marigold*. After best wishes, both Colonels accompanied the Captain to the general office so he could thank the office force for catering to all the *Marigold*'s needs.

Back aboard, Ray Fosse and Dick Richings were waiting on the bridge to let the Captain know that car transportation to Seattle had been arranged for the three of them the next afternoon.

Each happening, each remark intensified the reality of the final curtain. It came with the arrival of Captain Asa Harris, the relieving master, to take over the ship by signing for the ship's documents. December 15,

1945 ended Captain Skalley's service to the *Marigold*. The act of giving up the ship brought on a strong feeling of loss, but tempered by one of satisfaction, a loss in that the bond between ship and master was over and satisfaction that the ship had successfully carried out her mission. She could rest on her laurels.

Not all the staff had left by morning. Kathryn Adams with three other smiling nurses who the Captain held in high regard came up to his office and with a flourish presented him a set of the campaign ribbons and battle stars the ship had earned. They held both the Captain's hands and said they wouldn't forget the work and the worry that was his in keeping them afloat and if he ever needed nurses on any of his ships to call and they would come running! The Captain, deeply moved at the display of affection and showing it, thanked each one, "If I do need nurses or nursing, I'll make sure I need four. And don't forget we've been related ever since you became daughters of Neptune!"

Shortly after noon, the Captain, Ray Fosse and Dick Richings—all in uniform—walked down the gangway. At the bottom the Captain turned, raised his arm—encircled with four gold bands—saluted the flag, remembered the Women's Clubs and their part, then saluted the ship and—with a final wave to the remaining crew at the rail to see him off—he stepped into the waiting car. There wasn't any show of emotion; it was all inside. There would be many other ships, but only one *Marigold*.

SHIP'S CREW

DECK DEPARTMENT

CAPTAIN ROBERT M. SKALLEY	Master
RAYMOND E. FOSSE	First Officer
ROY L. ROBECK	Second Officer
REX E. HARWOOD	Third Officer
JOSEPH L. LaFRENIERE	Third Officer
DONALD C. MacKAY	Jr. 3rd Officer
FREDERICK MATTHEWS	Jr. 3rd Officer
RICHARD RICHINGS	Jr. 3rd Officer

SIXTO G. AVILLA	Carpenter
CARL P. McGEE	Boatswain
ROBERT A. McGILLIS	Carp. Mate
RODNEY GRAHAM	Deck Yeoman
HARRY DOLLEY	Wheelman
JOHN L. PARKER	Wheelman
JOHN WESTERHOLD	Wheelman
SIDNEY WHITING	Wheelman
ARTHUR P. DOME	Dk. Storekeeper
RICHARD ALASCANO	AB Seaman
ELMER BAUSCHKE	AB Seaman
BERT V. CHURCH	AB Seaman
ROGER CRUMP	AB Seaman
WILLIAM CRUMP	AB Seaman
DONALD DAWES	AB Seaman
CHARLES HIDEY	AB Seaman
JAMES LEWIS	AB Seaman
JAMES McGARRIGLE	AB Seaman
FREDERICO ESMUNDO	AB Seaman
NORMAN NENOFF	AB Seaman
RICHARD THOMPSON	AB Seaman
THEODORE WIEDEMANN	AB Seaman
MARVIN YOUNG	AB Seaman
WILLIAM H. DIXON	Ord. Seaman
JOSE L. RAZON	Ord. Seaman
ROBERT MURPHY	Ord. Seaman
RICHARD SLEEPER	Ord. Seaman
JACK TEETERS	Ord. Seaman
KENNETH KING	Ord. Seaman

TRANSPORTATION OFFICE

MAX H. FAUST	Transportation Agent
ROBERT SPRAGUE	Transportation Clerk
WAYNE P. O'DAY	Transportation Clerk
THOMAS A. JOHNSON	Transportation Clerk
JAMES D. HARTZOG	Transportation Clerk

OFFICER PERSONNEL OF THE 212TH HOSPITAL SHIP COMPLEMENT

ADAMS, LORRAINE K.,	Mapelton, Minn.
ANDERSON, ORLIN	Rib Lake, Minn.
BARR, MILDRED L.	Lowell, Wash.
BOLAN, GERTRUDE M.	Sacramento, Calif.
BORUM, VAUNDA M.	Aberdeen, Wash.
BRYAN, FAY	Barbourville, W. VA.
BEEBE, KENNETH H.	Sterling, Colo.
CAREY, MARGARET P.	East Grand Fords, Minn.
CLAUSEN, ETHEL C.	Denver, Colo.
CONNELL, JUNE L.	Camden, S.C.
DONAHOE, MARY E.	Sedalia, MO.
EKEREN, WALTER A.	Thief River Falls, Minn.
DORAN, FRANCES E.	Pittsfield, Mass.
FRANCOIS, RUTH E.	Centralia, Ill.
GAYNES, LEONARD	Chicago, Ill.
GAZELLA, BETTY	Owasso, Mich.
GRADINGER, ARNOLD S.	Brooklyn, N.Y.
GRIEP, MAE E.	Baker, Ore.
GRZESKOWIAK, ALICE C.	Milwaukee, Wisc.
GRZESKOWIAK, FLORENCE M.	Milwaukee, Wisc.
GORE, MARJORE F.	Yakima, Wash.
HOEFEL, WILMA E.	Billico, Calif
HORSLEY, ROBERTA	Waitsburg, Wash.
JONES, PAUL L.	Salt Lake City, Utah
KASER, JOSEPHINE H.	Los Angeles, Calif.
KOOK, EDNA M.	Los Angeles, Calif.
KNEUBEL, OLLIE E.	Long Island, Kansas
LANNING, HARVEY O.	Lexington, N.C.
LAKIN (SPENCER) LUCILLE	Denver, Colo.
LENNART, LUCILLE E.	Everson, Wash.
MIECZKOWSKI, STEPHEN P.	Milwaukee, Wisc.
MOREHEAD, MARY L.	Rulo, Nebraska
MURIN, FRANK A.	Chicago, Ill.
MURRILL, BEATRICE M.	Richmond, Calif.
OETKEN, TENNIE M.	San Antonio, Texas
PADWISOCKA, LOUIS K.	Brooklyn, N.Y.
PITTARD, HARRY A.	Little Rock, Ark.
POTTER, VIOLA	Freeport, Maine
RISDALL, ESTHER L.	Hinckley, Minn.
ROBINSON, MILDRED L.	Berkeley, Calif.
ROSS, MAURICE	Biddeford, Maine
RUFSVOLD, CLARICE A.	Ft. Ransom, N.D.
SATERBAK (SYMMES) GLADYS	Wheaton, Minn.
SCHULDT, HERTHA M.	Lakefield, Minn.
SCHULTZ, CLAIRE J.	San Diego, Calif.
SCHWARTZ, DORIS K.	Brooklyn, N.Y.
SCHOWENGERDT, WILLIAM R.	Champaign, Ill.
SENKFOR, WILLIAM	Cleveland, Ohio
STEWART, DONN W.	Ontario, Calif.
STYPUL, MARY M.	Harvey, Ill.
SHUSTER, HELEN B.	Park City, Mont.
TERRY, LUCILLE	E. Alton, Ill.
TIPTON, HELEN B.	Paola, Kansas
WILKINS, HARRY J.	Waukesha, Wisc.
WATKINS, WALTER C.	Amarillo, Texas
WHITESITT, JOYCE	Stevensville, Mont.
WOOLDRIDGE, WILFRED E.	Springfield, Mo.
ZICK, LUTHER H.	Albion, Mich.

ENGINE DEPARTMENT

L. SORENSEN	Chief Engineer
C.W. SPENCE	1st Asst. Engineer
STANLEY KOJAC	2nd Asst. Engineer
T.J. McGLOTHLIN	3rd Asst. Engineer
FREDERICK SESTAK	3rd Asst. Engineer
HENRY C. GEPKE	Jr. 3rd Asst.
ROBERT PEMBERTON	Jr. 3rd Asst.
JOHN A. GREGORICH	Jr. 3rd Asst.
OGDEN ROGERS	Jr. 3rd Asst.
H.M. SWIFT	Eng. Yeoman
W.C. ROBBINS	Chief Elec.
JESS ANDERSON	Asst. Elec.
CLARENCE ALVIS	Asst. Elec.
JAMES GUSTAFSON	Asst. Elec.
S.C. St.CLAIR	Reefer Eng.
P.E. GALLAGHER	Reefer Eng.
STANLEY WHITE	Reefer Eng.
LEON PIESCO	Plumber
LOUIS JONES	Plumber
O. SOUTHERLAND	Deck Eng.
ALVIN BOONE	Utility
WILLIAM HAMPTON	Storekeeper
CLIFFORD MANNING	Watertender
JOHN J. GAUGHAN	Watertender
ROY L. BAY	Watertender
ERIC AXELSON	Oiler
GEORGE GALLOWAY	Oiler
C. JASUKEWCZ	Oiler
CHARLES NELSON	Oiler
EDWARD TESAR	Oiler
WILLIAM HOHMAN	Oiler
GERALD CALHOUN	Oiler
L.K. ANDERSON	Oiler
RONALD DAUZAT	Fireman
HOWARD DYE	Fireman
R. BUKOVICH	Fireman
ARTHUR AVANT	Fireman
ROBERT QUINN	Fireman
A. WINKLER	Fireman
R. MARTIN	Wiper
HARVEY BAKER	Wiper
FREDERICK BUCK	Wiper
ODON ANCAJAS	Wiper

STEWARD DEPARTMENT

WALTER J. PRECHT	DAN SYMMES
"Chief Steward"	"2nd. Steward"
HOKE THOMAS	JOHN BUTCHER
"3rd. Steward"	"Chief Cook"
CALVIN DUKE	EUTIQUIANO GOMEZ
"2nd. Cook"	"2nd. Cook"
CARL LIVELY	FRED OLIVERA
"2nd. Cook"	"2nd. Cook"
JACK CAMPBELL	MONSON MARTENEZ
"3rd. Cook	"3rd. Cook"
OSCAR SUTTON	RALPH HUBBARD
"3rd. Cook"	"Chief Baker"
HARLAND HOUSEHOLTER	JOSE SANTOS
"2nd. Baker"	"2nd. Baker"
FLORENTINO FERNANDEZ	BENHART GEHLEN
"3rd. Baker"	"Chief Butcher"
BEN GEHLEN	KLESMER LOWRY
"2nd. Butcher"	"2nd. Butcher"
JAMES COBLENTZ	JOHN ARTEMKO
"Chief Storekeeper"	"Asst. Storekeeper"

STEWARD DEPARTMENT (Cont'd)

CHARENCE MARTINEAU
"Yeoman"
RAFAEL AGTUCA
"Chief Pantryman"
LUIS EARNSHAW
"2nd. Pantryman"
WILLIAM SCHIERBECKER
"Utilityman"
LESTER ROHN
"Night Watchman"
RAMOND EARNSHAW
"Utilityman"
CEFERINO DEMAYUGA
"Room Steward"
VALENTINE ARRASTIA
"Messman"
ARMANDO PORRAS
"Messman"
MANUEL SAN JUAN
"Messman"
ALBERT LEVI
"Messman"
JUAN SAMSON
"Messman"
SALVADOR De La ROSA
"Messman"
LEONARD FERRANDEZ
"Waiter"
FRED VEA
"Waiter"
THOMAS ALDEQUER
"Utility"
JOSE GUTTIERREZ
"Utility"
RICHARD NIDEVER
"Utility"

NICETAS GONZALES
"Linenman"
VICTORINE PIPO
"2nd. Pantryman"
WILLARD MATTSON
"Utilityman"
ANGEL ALDEQUER
"Night Watchman"
BRUCE FINNEY
"Utilityman"
HOMER WINE
"Utilityman"
RICARDO BUMANGLAG
"Messman"
ALFONSO CABE
"Messman"
ANTHONY SANZ
"Messman"
RENATO SAN JUAN
"Messman"
ALFRED SKILES
"Messman"
EDDIE VARGAS
"Messman"
JAMES De' ALTONGA
"Messman"
MIGUEL PERILLA
"Waiter"
FRANK BRU
"Waiter"
JOSE TUMACDER
"Utility"
ORLYN REEK
"Utility"
EDUARDO SANIDAD
"Utility"

ENLISTED MEN

ALTADONNA, PASQUALE J.	Brooklyn, New York
ACKERSON, CLARENCE	Cedar Falls, Iowa
ALEXANDER, ALVY	San Antonio, Texas
ANTHONY, THOMAS G.	San Francisco, Calif.
ARMAN, ROBERT S.	Toledo, Ohio
BAUER, SYLVESTER W.	East Eden, New York
BECKWITH, AL J.	Spokane, Wash.
BENNY, KENNETH	Chehalis, Wash.
BERNARDO, FRED F.	New Haven, Conn.
BERNSTEIN, NAT	New York, New York
BERRY, MILTON L.	Buford, Georgia
BLAKE, ULYS E.	Greeneville, Tennessee
BOSTWICK, HAROLD O.	Chattanooga, Oklahoma
BOTTLE, JAMES M.	Greene, New York
BOYSEN, JOHN P.	Peublo, Colorado
BRANCO, ANTONIO F.	North Tarrytown, N. Y.
BRACHLE, HAROLD J.	Denver, Colorado
BROCK, RALPH J.	Kansas City, Mo.
BUCHER, ALBERT W.	Bellaine, Michigan
BULLOCK, ROBERT B.	Los Angeles, Calif.
CABRERA, JOE	Arroyo Grande, Calif.
CALCAGNO, CARMEN	Chicago, Illinois
CASH, MACK	Forestburg, Texas
CALDWELL, ROBERT E.	Salina, Kansas
CANNARIATO, WILLIAM S.	Passaic, New Jersey
CARLOCK, WALTER A.	Paynesville, Minnesota
CARLSON, ROBERT T.	Kylertown, Pennsylvania

CARROLL, PATRICK J.	Chicago, Illinois
CHESTER, JOHN G.	Granite Falls, North Carolina
CLARK, HARRY H.	Henderson, North Carolina
CLARK, ROBERT L.	Mulberry, Indiana
CLAYTON, WILLIAM C.	Bridgeport, Conn.
COHEN, JOSEPH	New York, New York
COLE, ANTHONY	Grand Rapids, Michigan
CORNELLA, JOEY V.	Frontenac, Kansas
CUCHIE, FRANK	Elizabeth, New Jersey
CURCIO, RAFAELE M.	Brooklyn, New York
DAVIS, FRANK	Arcata, California
DOLAN, EDWARD R.	Middletown, New York
DZWIGONSKI, ADAM S.	Chicago, Illinois
ENGLAND, ALPHA L.	Sparta, Tennessee
ENNIS, HARRY H.	Provo, Utah
ERHARD, GEORGE A.	Scalp Level, Pennsylvania
FISHER, WILLIAM J.	Pittsburgh, Pa.
FLINN, RICHARD H.	Twin Falls, Idaho
FREISLEBEN, JOHN F.	Santa Barbara, Calif.
FRISBIE, ERNEST E.	Amarillo, Texas
FOLINO, ANTONIO T.	Wall, Pa.
FUTCH, RAY	Hahira, Georgia
GABRIEL, LOUIS	Youngstown, Ohio
GILLEN, WAYNE B.	Springfield, Illinois
GILLESPIE, GRANT M.	Akron, Ohio
GIROLAMI, ARMANDO	Rennselaer, New York
GNUSCHKE, HERMAN C.	Cosby, Missouri
GRANGER, ROGER P.	Charlette, Michigan
GREEN, FRANK T.	Quannah, Texas
GREEN, JOSEPH H.	Willoughby, Ohio
GRONER, JOE	Chicago, Illinois
HAGERMAN, ROBERT B.	Houlton, Maine
HANNON, CHARLES W.	Tampa, Florida
HANSEN, WALTER F.	Chicago, Illinois
HAMMOND, CLAUDE C.	Chicago, Illinois
HARRISON, WILFRED D.	Alpena, Michigan
HAYNES, JAMES K.	Gate City, Virginia
HAYMER, OSCAR	Del Water Gap, Pennsylvania
HENDERSON, DELMAR L.	Goodland, Indiana
HENDRIX, DONALD E.	Burbank, Calif.
HANKS, R.B.	Mill Valley, California
HEPPLER, WILLIAM P.	Philadelphia, Pa.
HICKSON, HUBERT H.	Colorado, Texas
HILL, BERNARD B.	Elgin, Illinois
HILLER, ALBERT	Brooklyn, New York
HOKE, FRANK	E. Stroudsburg, Pa.
HOWARD, BRYCE R.	North Powder, Oregon
IPSON, CHESTER W.	Cmargo, Oklahoma
JACKSON, LEE ALLEN	Leedey, Oklahoma
JIMMERSON, CHALMAGE C.	Boaz, Alabama
JOHNSTON, DONALD C.	Sandusky, Michigan
JUSTYNSKI, CHESTER F.	Hammond, Indiana
KATZ, HENRY	Baltimore, Maryland
KIBLER, ELMER C.	Mayville, North Dakota
KIME, EDWARD C.	Detroit, Michigan
KIRBY, CARLIE P.	Franklin, Ky.
KOROLIA, MIKE M.	New Orlenas, Louisiana
KOROTAJ, ALBERT S.	Los Gatos, California
LANG, CARROLL W.	Sand Point, Idaho
LEEPART, CHARLES R.	Warrensville, Ohio
LOOBY, GEORGE W.	St. Louis, Missouri
LUCAS, FRANK	Chicago, Illinois
McCLELLAND, WALTER L.	Waynesburg, Pa.
McCURRY, CLYDE A.	Chicota, Texas
McDONALD, ROY E.	Akron, Ohio
McKENZIE, EUGENE D.	McMinnville, Oregon
MARAOLDO, OSWALDO	New York, New York
MARTINEZ, FERMIN	Yuma, Arizona

MASON, EDWARD W.	Meriden, Conn.
MEREDITH, FRANK J.	Birmingham, Ala.
MEYER, IRA W.	Louisville, Ky.
MEYERS, SUMNER D.	Mattapan, Mass.
MILLER, CLARENCE	Egg Harbor, New Jersey
MILLS, RAYMOND E.	Chicago, Illinois
MIRES, EARL D.	Dallas, Texas
MISKELLY, WILLIAM J.	Sebring, Ohio
MODAFFERI, PAUL	Brooklyn, New York
MOORE, JOHN W.	Sacramento, California
MORGANTI, FRANK J.	Oakland, Calif.
MORTON, ROY E.	Boston, Mass
MURPHY, JULIAN V.	Danville, Va.
NEFF, EDWARD I.	Fort Ashby, West Virginia
NILL, WILLIAM	New York, New York
NIXON, GERALD R.	Canton, Ohio
O'CONNER, JAMES E.	Worchester, Mass.
O'NEILL, JACK	Columbus, Ohio
OURSO, CHARLES C.	Plaque Mine, Louisiana
ORTEGA, JOHN C.	Salt Lake City, Utah
OWENS, DALE K.	Buhl, Idaho
PAYNE, DONALD E.	Rush Springs, Oklahoma
PECORELLI, VINCENT	Stratford, Conn.
PIERCE, JOHN H.	Milton, Mass
PIPER, ROYDON C.	Altoona, Pa.
PITTMAN, JAMES N.	Rose Field, Louisiana
POMEROY, VERNON	Colorado Springs, Colo.
PROCHASKA, ERWIN	Fairfield, Conn.
PROND, MELVIN G.	Toledo, Ohio
QUAACK, JESS W.	Louisville, Ky.
RICHARDS, JOHN K.	Seattle, Wash.
RIVERA, MIQUEL E.	Riverside, Calif.
RODDY, CHARLES E.	Dayton, Ohio
ROSA, MICHAEL J.	Cambridge, Mass.
ROUBIQUE, PHILIBERT	Baton Rouge, La.
RUIZ, ROBERT B.	Fort Worth, Texas
RUTH, GEORGE E.	E. Stroudburg, Pa.
SAND, DONALD	Rochester, New York
SAWYER, CHARLES	Cincinnati, Ohio
SCHNAUTZ, RALPH E.	Saginaw, Michigan
SELLERS, DWIGHT L.	Lyman, Wyoming
SHAHDAN, KAISER	Fall River, Mass.
SHOAF, ROBERT L.	Cameron, Texas
SILVA, JOHN C.	Colton, California
SMITH, ALLEN L.	Buffalo, New York
SMITH, ROBERT E.	Morristown, New Jersey
SMITH, SHIRLEY K.	Port Huron, Michigan
SPEAKS, JOHN L.	Portland, Oregon
STAGNER, JAMES L.	Seattle, Wash.
STANDLEY, ANDREW R.	Perkins, Missouri
STANIGER, LAWRENCE	Chisholm, Minn.
STEENBURG, E.A.	Aurora, Nebraska
STOECKLE, JAMES T.	St. Joseph, Mo.
STRUG, JOSEPH J.	Detroit, Michigan
TALLMAN, KENNETH V.	Dallas, Texas
THOMAS, BERNARD D.	Washington, D.C.
THOMPSON, ARTHUR J.	Normandy, St. Louis, Mo.
THUL, DONALD J.	Chicago, Illinois
TINTO, JOSEPH H.	Brookfield Center, Conn.
TURSI, MICHAEL J.	Philadelphia, Pa.
VELLA, PETER	New York, New York
VILLAREAL, JOSE R.	San Antonio, Texas
VIPOND, FLOYD E.	Loma Linda, California
WATSON, KERMIT J.	Banks, Arkansas
WELENC, WALLACE	Archbald, Pa.
WILLIAMS, SHERLEY	Madison, Illinois
WITMER, JOHN V.	Comunbia, Pa.
YOUNG, FLOYD F.	Lincoln, Nebraska

Author's Note:

For the information of those people involved
with the Marigold directly or vicariously, the ship
entered the reserve fleet at Suisun Bay—San
Francisco, California in 1946, and two years later
was sold for dismantling.